A Place for People, Puppets, and Cockroach Soup

A Place for People, Puppets, and Cockroach Soup

Pioneering Delightfully Over-the-Top and Seriously Under-Budgeted Christian TV Productions

by Margaret (Maggie) Register

Printed by CreateSpace

Copyright © 2012 by Margaret A. Register

A Place for People, Puppets, and Cockroach Soup:
Pioneering Delightfully Over-the-Top and Seriously Under-Budgeted
Christian TV Productions

by Margaret A. Register

Printed in the United States of America

ISBN 978-1470122836

All rights reserved solely by the author. The author guarantees all contents are original and do not infringe upon the legal rights of any other person or work. No part of this book may be reproduced in any form without the permission of the author. The views expressed in this book are not necessarily those of the publisher.

Unless otherwise noted, Scripture quotations are taken from the HOLY BIBLE, NEW INTERNATIONAL VERSION®. NIV®.Copyright © 1973,1978, 1984, 2002 by International Bible Society.
Used by permission of Zondervan.
All rights reserved.

Drawings preceding each chapter are from the *Secret Place* Coloring Book designed by Judith Bartel Graner. *Used by permission of author.*

Cover design by Tim Register

Sequel to
No Place for Plastic Saints: Earthquakes,
Chicken Feet, and Candid Confessions
of a Missionary Wife

Dedication

A writer needs a pen,
An artist needs a brush,
But a filmmaker needs an army.
—*Orson Welles*

This book is dedicated to the hundreds of volunteers who, for 26 years, from 1978 - 2004, "made" STAR Ministries. They gave of themselves, their talents, and their resources. In fact, they actually built the studio: they put up the steel beams; framed-in the rooms; installed drywall; laid tile; laid carpet; papered hallways; sawed, hammered, painted, plumbed, and prayed.

Volunteers designed and built sets for the television shows. They set-up and tore-down the sets for "shoot" after "shoot." They ran audio cables, operated cameras, and adjusted lights. They sewed costumes; they dressed and operated puppets. They applied make-up on "live" people, and cooked delicious meals for the cast and crew.

Listed below and on the following page are the names of a few of these people whose selfless acts made possible the ministry of *Spanish Television And Radio:*

A	Al, Ann, Annie, Aretha, Andrea, Andrés, Andrew, April, Amanda, Ana, Anna, Amy, Austin
B	Bill, Bob, Brad, Bruce, Brandon, Barry, Brian, Bea, Betty, Barbara, Billy
C	Cheryl, Carol, Carole, Carlos, Curt, Clarence, Carla, Cara, Connie, Chris, Christine, Charles, Charlie, Cleo, Calvin, Cory
D	Dottie, Doug, Dan, Dana, Danielle, David, Dave, Dolores, Deborah, Doris, Don, Donald, Donnie, Drew, DesiRee, Donna Lee, Dean, Dianne, Darla, Dara, Dorothy, Dennis, DeAndre
E	Edwina, Ed, Eugene, Eva, Elizabeth, Eldon, Emily
F	Floyd, Fred, Frieda, Fredda, Francine, Frances, Frank

G	Gerry, Glenn, Gayle, Glendon, Greg, Ginger, Gerald, Grace, Glynis, Gloria, Gary, Guy, George
H	Hilda, Holly, Harold, Howard, Herman, Henry, Haley, Hanna, Heidi, Heather
I	Israel
J	Jerry, June, Jennifer, Jenny, Judy, Judi, Jim, Josh, Joey, Jack, Juan, Jan, Joy, John, Jero, Janie, Jessica, Janine, Jonathan, James, Jeremy, Joani, Jacque, Jason, Jared, Jasmine, Jonaira
K	Ken, Kim, Kyndal, Karen, Kendra, Kerri, Katie, Kathy
L	Lorraine, Lorene, Layna, Lisa, Larry, Lynn, Linda, Louise, Libia
M	Mary, Maritza, Mike, Mark, Maxine, Matt, Michael, Margo, Melody, Mel, Myrt, Melanie, Marian, Marlin, Marla, Margaret, Mia, Matthew
N	Nelsa, Nelda, Neil, Noni
O	Opal, Olan
P	Paula, Paul, Pearl, Paulette
R	Red, Ronnie, Ruth, Randy, Rick, Ryan, Ron, Ray, Russ, Roger, Rachel, Raquel, Regina, Rebekah, Roberto, Rita
S	Sara, Sheila, Steve, Scott, Shelby, Susie, Shaun, Shawn, Scrivner, Shirley, Sandra, Shiloh, Stephanie, Shanna, Sue
T	Tammy, Tom, Tim, Terry, Traci
V	Victor
W	William, Wade, Wayne, Winnie, Woody, Wilma, Wanda
Y	Yolanda

Preface

What a delight to be able to tell what God has done through ordinary people who joined their energies and prayers to produce Christian videos for children, adolescents, and adults. Creativity flowed freely through the studio and saturated every location where we "shot."

When I wrote this book, distinctive people "came to mind" as illustrations of the different time frames of STAR's development. I've entitled chapters after these people; however, the chapters also present various other people and ongoing events of that particular time frame.

We began to pioneer STAR Ministries in 1978 never dreaming that God would bring so many people—and puppets—into our lives and our ministry. Productions flourished as people whom God touched on the shoulder came to join the team for long or short periods.

Someone compared us to a train speeding down the track with people getting on board at station after station. Since those early days, distribution has continued; today, it reaches even farther than ever before.

But I'm getting ahead of myself. I hope you enjoy this story!

Margaret (Maggie) Register

TV Terms

Cameraman – the person who operates the camera (used for both male and female camera operators); the cameraman "runs camera," as in "Evelyn, are you available to run camera next week?"

Cast – the people in front of the camera (whom the viewer sees)

Crew – everyone behind the scenes, all the technical people

Cut – a command to stop filming; also, one "take" of a scene: "How many cuts do we have of her kissing the cat before it scratched her on the face?"

Director – the person in charge of the filming

Editor – the person who pieces together all the elements of a completed show; he or she determines how quickly the final product seems to move by making tight or loose edits; adds sound effects; adds music under; enhances the video; adds text to the screen; drinks lots of coffee or Coke and puts in very long hours

Film – noun: actually, we used only videotape, so we tried always to say "tape"

Film – verb: to record

Final Cut Pro – a professional editing program on the computer; the standard for professionals

Floor – "the floor" is the area indoors, in the studio, where the filming takes place

Floor director – the person who tells the talent what to do; reassures the talent; conveys the director's wishes to the talent (softens the instructions from "Tell him TO STAND on the X!" to "Sir, be sure to stop here, on the X this time, OK? You can do it, you're doing great.")

Format – the flow of the show; the style; also, the written order of the show segments

Grid – the "lighting grid" is a network of pipes, overhead, to hold the studio lights

Host, hostess – the person on camera who greets the viewer and interacts with the other talent

Light the set – to place powerful lights in strategic places to illuminate the scene

Lit the set – indicates that the set has good lighting on it and is ready to roll tape

Log – a written account of the scenes, their length, what tape number each scene is recorded on

Platforms – three feet high collapsible, wooden tables that become the puppet's floor, when the puppet is held high in the air

Presenter – the person who teaches or "presents" the lesson that is being recorded

Producer – the person who conceptualizes the show or series; he chooses the director to carry out his wishes

Props – items needed "on set," such as a telephone or rubber snake, or Bobo's plastic roaches

Puppeteer – the person who holds the puppet and manipulates its mouth, hands, and body; the puppeteer gives voice and personality to the puppet; he individualizes it by adding specialized clothing (such as a baseball cap); he imagines a "back story" to add dimension to the puppet's life and personality

Record – verb: to put the show onto videotape

Roll tape – record the program

Script – the written dialogue with personality descriptions for the actors; includes essential movements (such as "pushes the wheelchair down the stairs")

Set – the scene the camera "sees," for example, a couch and chair beside a fireplace

Set the lights – hang big lights so they shine on the scene

Shoot – noun: what you intend to record; "We have a shoot scheduled for Monday."

Shoot – verb: to record the scene

Show – what is being, or has been recorded onto video or audio tape, "the show"

Spot – a commercial, usually 15, 30 or 60 seconds in length

Stand by – get focused, be alert, we're almost ready to shoot

Studio – the area designated for filming; the sets are there; the ceiling is high; the lights are there on poles or hanging on a grid overhead

Take – a recording of a scene; many times there are various "takes" of the same action

Talent – the people who are the actors or presenters

Tape – the actual videotape or the process of "taping" or filming

That's a wrap – we have finished this segment; that's all we're recording right now

Videographer – an accomplished cameraman who also knows lighting and audio

Contents

Prologue: Bobo

Page	
1	Pastor Waldron
7	Fredda
9	Algernon
15	Eva
21	Paul
25	Juan
31	Bob
35	John
39	Sue
45	Cristina
51	David T.
55	Maritza and Sarita
67	David L.
75	Carl
83	Bruce
87	Roland
93	Evelyn
97	Hilda
103	Bobo's Favorite Recipes
115	Red, Ed, and Fred-da
125	Tim
135	Toni
147	Dottie and Ken
155	Neil
165	Judy
173	Ana
185	Frieda
199	Carol
205	Isaac
213	Maggie
225	Gene and Jeanne
255	Bobby
261	Mario
269	A Word from Joe

Pages from the *Secret Place Coloring Book* are used as illustrations in this book.

Prologue: Bobo

Guatemala 1987

Joe's heart lurched. Sweat beaded his brow. He would be trampled! Just in front of him stood the wire, double gate of the stadium. It was bowing toward him as thousands of children pushed against it. How could Joe escape being crushed by the crowd? Then to his right he saw a small opening under the lip of the concrete bleachers. He scurried into it. Just in time. The gates opened. The crowd surged into the stadium.

Outside, the smells of food cooking on a dozen hibachis mingled with the shouts of vendors. Roasted meat, ice cream, Coca-Cola. With legs spraddled and colorful skirts tucked firmly around their knees, women squatted beside the hibachis. Carefully tending the smoking coals, the women turned pieces of beef and pork and chicken. Men carried flat, wooden boxes of merchandise—Chicle gum and candy bars and Pez-like candy squares—balanced against their bellies, the open boxes suspended on straps strung behind their necks. Other vendors, pushing ice cream carts along the cobblestones, rang small bells to hawk their wares.

Hundreds of children and parents continued to arrive, pushing and shoving to establish a place in line. The queue grew, broadened, and stretched down the street to the highway, then along the highway as far as we could see.

Back inside, Joe watched thousands of children scramble up onto the bleachers of the basketball stadium in Guatemala City. Boys in dark blue uniforms attempted to act as ushers to the burgeoning crowd. Girls in light blue uniforms tried to help smaller children find seats.

Standing in line to see Bobo

The line stretched around the stadium
and down the street

Lugar Secreto was here! Today! The people from STAR Ministries—the entire cast of the famous television show—were here! Clowns danced on the stage and along the stadium floor to entertain the kids as they waited for the show to begin.

Tingles of excitement spread through the crowd. Sparkling eyes flitted across the stage. Suddenly, a voice chanted, "Bo-bo. Bo-bo." Another voice joined in. A dozen voices. A hundred voices. A thousand. Two. Three. *Six* thousand voices yelling, "¡Bo-bo! ¡Bo-bo!"

Inside the stadium

Two hours later, a second crowd of 6,000 children chanted to begin the show. And two hours after that, 6,000 *more* children chanted to begin the *third* show.

Tears ran down Joe's cheeks. For twenty years he had been a missionary. He had preached in conventional ways. He had established churches and taught in Bible colleges throughout Latin America. But never had he reached so many people at one time. Never did he dream that a puppet, *his* puppet, would touch so many lives, or that 18,000 children would come to see *Bobo*.

Where did Joe get this puppet? And why?

Why did he name the puppet "Bobo"?

Why did so many kids come to see Bobo?

What is this television show called *Lugar Secreto*?

And how did it begin?

Who wrote the scripts, created the sets, and operated the numerous puppets?

Where did the funding come from?

The cast and crew were from *STAR Ministries*? What in the world is *STAR Ministries*?

"HI! WELCOME TO SECRET PLACE."
¡HOLA, AMIGUITO! ¡BIENVENIDO AL "LUGAR SECRETO"!

"DEAR LORD, BLESS MY COCKROACH SOUP!"
"¡QUERIDO SEÑOR, BENDICE MI SOPA DE CUCARACHAS!"

1

Pastor Waldron

May we? Can we?

June 1977

    The traffic seemed awfully quiet as we drove away from the Tampa International Airport to the nearest McDonald's. No horns blowing, no black smoke billowing. Traffic lights dotted major intersections. Stop signs stood guard on corners. Asphalt sang beneath the car tires as we glided along smooth roads without huge potholes. No pedestrians crowded the streets; no military personnel dotted the roadway with soldiers' bright buttons shining, their polished carbines slung over a shoulder. What a change it was from Paraguay!
    The restaurant gleamed with clean tables and an unlittered floor. Christy, fifteen, and Timmy, twelve, savored each bite of the French fries, dipping the salty tips into rich catsup. I held onto the Styrofoam container that had held my hamburger. I couldn't throw it away. Why did people throw away, so nonchalantly, these valuable storage containers? But Mavis, my sister-in-law, took it from me and tossed it into the trash.
    When I overheard some people speaking English, I stood—on impulse—and started to walk toward them, to introduce myself as a fellow expatriate. Suddenly, I stopped, as I realized we were back in the States. Speaking English was commonplace here!
    Joe and I, Christy and Timmy, had arrived from Paraguay only moments before, where we had just spent four years as missionaries.

We drove out of Tampa into the countryside, to Durant, Florida, where Kenny and Mavis, Joe's brother and sister-in-law, lived in a modest home on Turkey Creek Road. For a week, they hosted us, even taking us to Disneyworld. Our heads spun from seeing so many modern marvels, from observing the orderliness and organization of everything. The Disney streets were not littered with trash; the sidewalks were smooth and even. The rest rooms smelled clean and had toilet paper!

Our clothes, which had looked nice when we left Paraguay, now looked out-of-style and frumpy. Joe and the children had not been back to the States for four years, and I had made only one brief visit back when my nephew, Shawn, was born.

Everything we owned fit into our luggage and a small wooden crate. Before leaving Paraguay, we had sold or given away almost all our possessions. Basically, all we possessed now was a dream—Joe's dream of beginning a television ministry that could, possibly, touch all of Latin America.

After a few days, Joe asked Kenny if we could borrow his car to drive to visit Tom and Maxine Waldron, our first employers and friends from Beckley, West Virginia. They had retired in nearby Lakeland. Sitting in their living room, we relaxed and told stories while we remembered old times. We all laughed, especially at the story about Joe and me "having to get married" in order for Pastor Waldron to hire Joe as his Youth and Music Pastor. Tom Waldron had certainly changed our lives!

My thoughts went back to 1961; Joe had been a graduating senior at Southeastern University, in Lakeland, Florida. I was a freshman, so when we parted for the summer, we did not know when we would see each other again. That would be his last summer to travel with the school quartet throughout the southeast to youth camps and churches. After that, he would have to find a job.

In July, Joe went to the West Florida camp and the camp director asked him to lead the camp choir. Since I just "happened" to be there, Joe asked me to accompany the choir on the piano. We worked together during rehearsals and "trained" a four-part choir. We sang "Master, the Tempest is Raging," and it sounded like it!

The next week, Joe called the president of Southeastern to ask for more travel funds for the quartet, and the president said, "A pastor was just here looking for an associate. I recommended you. Give him a call."

So Joe called Tom Waldron, in Beckley, West Virginia. They talked for a while, and then Pastor Waldron said,

"Joe, as I've explained, I am looking for a youth pastor—music director. But I have several preliminary questions to ask you. First, have you ever directed a four-part choir?"

"Yes." (It was several years before Joe told him he'd had only three days of experience with a youth camp choir.)

"Second, can you type? Because I would need you to type up the church bulletin."

"Yes."

"Third, are you married? I won't hire a single guy—there are too many problems."

"I'm willing to be. Could I call you back?"

My phone rang. "Margaret, I have just been offered a job as an associate pastor!"

"Joe!"

"In Beckley, West Virginia."

"Joe!"

"They have a little parsonage for the associate!"

"Joe!"

"It's furnished, too."

"Joe!"

"The pastor asked me several questions and I have to call him back. If I get the job, can we get married?"

"Joe!"

"If I don't get the job, we can't get married."

"Can you call me back tomorrow?"

That night I opened my Bible to the place where I'd left off reading in Isaiah 30. Verse 21 leaped out at me: "This is the way, walk ye in it." I just knew, then, that *if* the job worked out, I should marry Joe.

Mom and Dad had no objection! They knew Pastor Waldron because they had ministered in West Virginia during their years of traveling with the evangelist, Roy Sherrill. They knew the church was large and stable. I was eighteen and could decide for myself, they said.

Joe called back. I said, "All right, let's go meet the pastor."

We arrived in Beckley on Saturday afternoon, met with Pastor Waldron, and he asked Joe and me to sing a duet on Sunday morning. He introduced us as "Joe and Margaret" without a last name, since we weren't married "yet." We sang the only duet we had learned together, "Heaven in My Heart."

Sunday afternoon, Pastor Waldron told us we were hired. We had two weeks to go back to Pensacola, get married, and be back at work! The pastor broadcast a daily radio program and produced a weekly television program; he needed Joe to help with both. However, Ira Stanphill would be in Beckley for a two-week revival and could provide the music in the meantime.

Joe went around telling all his college buddies we "had to get married." I teased him that he never did really "propose."

***

After four years in Beckley, we became pastors, then missionaries. We lived in Mexico, Chile, and Paraguay a total of ten years. (See my book *No Place for Plastic Saints: Earthquakes, Chicken Feet, and Candid Confessions of a Missionary Wife* for stories of our life there.)

***

But now, at this moment, Joe was not thinking of any of that—his mind was preoccupied as he tried to gain the courage to share, for the very first time, his new and probably impossible dream. But first, he needed to explain what had transpired in Paraguay.

"Pastor Waldron, you will not believe what happened in Paraguay. A few days after we arrived, Margaret and I, along with missionaries Roland and Evelyn Blount, sang on a television program. It was a 'special' show by Phil Saint, a visiting missionary-chalk-artist from Argentina. So many people commented on seeing us on the show that Roland and I decided to go down to the station and talk to the manager. To make a long story short, thirty-seven days after arriving in Asunción, we had a one-year contract for a weekly program—the first ever regularly scheduled evangelical program in the country!

"Rich people watched the show; poor people paid a small fee to their neighbors to watch TV with them. Soon the entire country knew Roland and me as 'the blind one and the bearded one' from *Las Buenas Nuevas* (*The Good News*) television program. Even the army—one time when they were bivouacked downtown in the park—saw us driving by and began to sing our theme song!"

Joe continued, "Pastor Waldron, during the four years we lived in Paraguay, hundreds of people would stop us to say, 'Your show is my favorite.'

"A few days ago, just before we left to come to the States, a woman called our house and asked if she could come to pray with us to receive Jesus as Savior. A shiny, black Mercedes pulled into our driveway. A uniformed chauffeur stepped out and opened the back door for a tiny, elegant, elderly lady. After the prayer, as *Doña Rebeca* prepared to leave, she paused at the front door, turned to me and said, 'Hermano José, we Paraguayans love the music on the television show. We love the way you read from the Bible. We enjoy the humor you display and the testimonies people give. But what speaks to our hearts, more than anything else, is the peace that we see on your faces.'

"Pastor Waldron, I wonder if, maybe, that was God's sign to me—because if television could have that much impact there, in one country …."

Joe took a ragged breath. He felt vulnerable and tentative, but he continued to unfold his dream: the desire to produce Christian television programming in Spanish; no preaching, but informal shows with lots of music, some Bible reading, and testimonies for all of Latin America. Joe swallowed, looked at the floor, and then said softly, "That's never been done before."

Without hesitation, Tom Waldron said, "Joe, look at me! You *can* do it. It *will* work. God has put this dream in your heart … He will help you to produce programs for all of Latin America!"

Joe's heart pounded while tears filled his eyes. He had dared to share his dream with his old mentor, and Pastor Waldron believed the dream was valid! We could have the courage to go forward.

Pastor Waldron murmured, "You know what? Karl Strader's church here in Lakeland has a television production truck, and they're supposed to receive some new equipment this week." He raised his voice, "Let's go down to Main Street. Right now!"

We walked into the church building to see a man kneeling on the floor of the hallway. He scattered Styrofoam pellets onto the floor as he lifted a new camera out of a box. Pastor Waldron explained who we were and why we were there. The man nodded, "I'm Paul Garber, director of the television department here. Joe, if you get permission to begin a TV ministry, I'll help you. I'll do all the technical part. You just produce the show in Spanish."

We were amazed! Could he really mean that? Would we be back in Lakeland someday?

2

Fredda

Could you use some puppets? For free?

August 1977

"Dad, Mom, you have to come and see the puppets! The woman tells me that she will give us a family of puppets—for free. Come on, pleeease," Christy begged every day.

After talking with Pastor Waldron, Joe contacted our Missions Board to share with them his dream of television productions. They said, "No, we've never approved a television ministry such as you envision. Why don't you move to Springfield, Missouri, attend graduate school, get your master's degree in Cross-Cultural Communications, and we'll consider this, maybe, next year?"

The Board believed Joe's dream would die. Later one of the men told us they had thought Joe was crazy. No one had ever done this. They believed no one could.

So, in the summer of 1977, we moved to Springfield, Missouri, where Joe would attend the graduate school. But our first duty was to attend a national church convention called *The General Council* in Oklahoma City.

Joe and I sat through business sessions while Christy and Timmy walked around through the exhibit area. All four of us felt weird, like misfits in this American culture. Pastors and delegates were dressed in the latest fashions. We didn't even know what the latest fashions were. And we didn't have money to shop for clothing for the entire family, even if we knew what to buy.

On the last afternoon of the Council, after Christy had pestered and pestered us, we followed her to the exhibit hall to meet "the puppet lady," Fredda Marsh. We did not believe she would actually give us puppets. It was probably a trick of some sort, to pull parents over to her booth, so the woman could give us a sales pitch.

A bright smile beamed from a round face. Fredda introduced herself and greeted us warmly. It was obvious that she treasured her puppets as if they were her children. She handed Joe a large, rectangular box. "Free to missionaries," she said. "My husband, Jim, passed away last month. I almost didn't attend this convention ... but he helped me make these puppets ... and he would want you to have these—a mom, a dad, a boy and a girl. I made these puppets out of brown fabric, so they would be brown-skinned like the people in Latin America."

We thanked her and walked away. On the drive back home, Christy and Timmy played with the puppets in the car. They made the little boy and girl "come alive," waving to passengers in other vehicles and making people smile.

But then, we put the puppets in their box in a closet and forgot all about them. We hardly remembered what the "puppet lady" looked like. It never occurred to us that we would ever see her again.

Algernon

Are we crazy or not?

We settled into life in Missouri. We found a small cottage to rent in "mission village," behind Central Bible College. The rent was low, as it should have been, because the place was pitiful, with dilapidated furniture. There were three tiny bedrooms, a tiny kitchen, and a small living room. The cottage sat in a row of similar old buildings formerly used for student housing.

Christy entered tenth grade. She was miserable. She didn't dress "right," she didn't talk "right." She didn't know anyone. She stood too close to other students—following the Paraguayan social norm. One day in her Home Economics class, Christy was handed a tube of biscuits. She had never heard of any such thing. The instructions said to hit the tube sharply against the edge of a table. She did, and biscuits went flying across the room, even hitting some of the other girls. And, of course, the girls laughed at her.

Every day Christy wore the same pair of jeans because they were the only thing "in style" that she owned. At the church youth group, Greg and Sandie Mundis were great youth pastors, but the kids there didn't interact as a group, playing games together as teens did in South America. Christy just didn't fit in anywhere.

Timmy entered junior high, seventh grade. He didn't know anyone in the large school. He was miserable. He didn't dress "right," he didn't talk "right." He was ashamed that he spoke Spanish. He didn't know how to play American football. Joe did take Timmy to buy a trombone and he actually enjoyed playing in beginner band, but he didn't really fit in anywhere.

I registered for classes at Central Bible College. But before school began—in fact, on the trip back from the convention in Oklahoma City, I began to hemorrhage heavily. Joe insisted that I see a doctor without delay. As I explained the condition I had already endured for many years, the doctor recommended major surgery and scheduled it immediately. New house, new classes, new culture, new gaping wound in my belly!

Joe registered at the graduate school (at this writing, called Assemblies of God Theological Seminary). It was as if every experience he'd ever had "came together" as he studied cross-cultural communications. Joe also composed a four-page, single-spaced prospectus for the Foreign Missions Committee. He delineated how his dream of television productions could become a reality.

Every month, Joe contacted our Director, Loren Triplett. "Do I have permission yet to begin a television ministry?" Every month Loren replied, "No. Impossible."

After several months of living in the tiny cottage with only one bathroom, I felt as if I would scream. One day when I came in from class, I opened the back door to find the old linoleum floor buried under a rusty-looking stream. I slogged inside and looked toward the living room: the worn carpet lay bloated; saturated with dirty water. That was the last straw! Please, God, let me move to a decent house!

Somehow we heard of a house for rent, nicely furnished, only a couple of blocks away. I could continue to walk to my classes at Central Bible College, and Christy could walk to Hillcrest High School. Timmy could walk home from Reed Junior High, too. We moved the next day, I think, leaving behind the broken pipes of an old, rusted-out water heater.

I loved the house on Kerr Street. There were three bedrooms, two baths, a garage, a lovely eat-in-kitchen with a bay window, a family room with a fireplace, and a formal living room.

And there was Algernon. He came home from school with Timmy one day. Algernon ran through the house, climbed up on the furniture, and made himself right at home. This beautiful white rat was so smart he could open his cage no matter how securely we closed it. Algernon loved to sneak out at night and burrow under the covers with Timmy, to sleep at his feet. Timmy had named the rat *Algernon* because he had studied at school the science fiction classic,

Flowers for Algernon by Daniel Keyes. Timmy knew *his* white rat would "stay intelligent" and would never regress the way the novel had depicted.

One morning, we could not find dear Algernon. He had managed to crawl up into the hide-a-bed sofa in the family room. We were afraid to open the sofa, for fear we'd squish him. We coaxed and coaxed, left a trail of food, and several nights later, he emerged, happily, and Timmy caught him.

Joe explained that Algernon needed his freedom ... so, reluctantly, Timmy took him to the far side of a large field across from our house and let him go free.

About a week later, our neighbor came over. "Hey, good news! I found your white rat. He was in my garage this morning." So Timmy, dragging his feet and his sad feelings of losing his pet, took Algernon back to school to find another kid who would love an adventuresome rat.

***

Recurring to Joe about that same time was an adventure he had experienced earlier when he had traveled to Venezuela to attend a three-day meeting of Latin American leaders. The accommodations in Caracas were adequate; the food—*pésima*—not so good. However, as Joe walked around preoccupied, his heart was troubled. The desire burned within him to produce television programs. But, would our Foreign Missions Committee ever approve of such a radical idea? And, was this project-idea *truly* necessary?

The second day of the convention, Joe accepted an invitation along with several other people to go to a missionary's high-rise apartment for an evening meal. Toward dusk, some of the people walked out onto the apartment's balcony. Spread out before them lay one of the most poverty-stricken barrios of Caracas. Poorly constructed shacks of tin and cardboard sat jammed together beside narrow dirt paths where sewage ran unabated. The missionary explained that even the police did not enter that barrio after dark. Soon, everyone except Joe wandered back inside the apartment. He stayed, staring at the barrio. He wept softly praying, "God, how could anyone ever hope to reach those people with the Gospel? It seems impossible."

Then, single, low-watt light bulbs began to twinkle on in numerous shacks. And bluish light began to spill out the open doorways. Suddenly Joe's heart thumped in his chest. For silhouetted against the skyline stood an army of TV antennas. These people had television sets! Joe learned later that most of these people had only one appliance and they would charge admission to their neighbors in order to make the monthly payment on their TV.

Standing on that hotel balcony, Joe whispered, "God, thank you. Thank you for cementing in my heart the dream you have given me. Thank you for this sign of confirmation. Someday, with your help, our programs will reach into *this very barrio!*"

***

And so, never forgetting that confirmation, Joe once again contacted our Director. "My dream is not dying—I still want permission to begin a television ministry." And this time, the Director said, "All right. Move to Lakeland. Try it. The Foreign Missions Committee will give you two years to see if you can get something going."

By the next day, fear had set in on four levels:

1. Ability—What if we really could not produce a Spanish show? Were we capable?
2. Acceptance from peers—If we could produce a show, would other missionaries accept it? Air it on local channels?
3. Acceptance from nationals—If we could produce a program, and it was aired, would national brothers accept it? Would they resent it? Or appreciate it?
4. Acceptance from viewers—If we could produce a program, and if the missionaries aired it, and if the national brothers accepted it, would anyone actually watch it?

The following Sunday morning Joe and I sat on a pew near the back of the church. We did not listen very well to the sermon because we were writing notes to each other, trying to come up with a name for the new venture. Missionary Television Productions. Spanish Television Shows. But we wanted to include radio productions, too. Spanish Television and Radio. S-T-A-R. Spanish Television and Radio! *STAR Productions.* Yes!

And so, with butterflies in our bellies, with fear-yet-hope in our hearts, with no money, with only a dream, we moved to Lakeland, Florida, on August 12, 1978.

We hoped Paul Garber meant what he had said! We hoped the invitation was still open! We hoped the church where he worked would welcome us. We hoped he would help us begin Spanish television and radio production!

Would we "run free" as our little Algernon had done (although ever so briefly)? Would our opportunity last? We knew that going out on our own into this new venture meant being risk-takers at a high level, but our hearts burned as we contemplated the impact our efforts *might* make in the then barely untapped avenue of Christian television in Latin America. Think of it—*STAR Productions*!

A Place for People, Puppets, and Cockroach Soup

FREDDA ASKS, "IS JESUS YOUR LORD AND SAVIOUR?"
FREDA PREGUNTA: "¿ES CRISTO TU SEÑOR Y SALVADOR?"

Eva

¿Puedo ayudarles?
May I help you?

September 1978

    I laughed until tears rolled down my cheeks. Eva Rodriguez and I ran, flipped cards, ran back to focus the television cameras, and ran forward to flip more cards onto the floor of the tiny television studio.

    We had met Eva at our new church home, First Assembly of God, located at 1350 East Main Street. Eva, with her husband and small children, had emigrated from Puerto Rico to Florida, and our first Sunday in Lakeland, she made a bee-line toward us as soon as church dismissed. She greeted us in Spanish and said she was there to serve us. Her Spanish grammar was excellent; she had earned a B.A. (in Spanish) in Theater and Drama. God sent Eva to help us!

    Earlier that morning, as soon as Joe and I, with Christy and Timmy, had walked into the church lobby, a woman approached us. Her eyes gleamed, her smile beamed, "Good morning! Welcome! I'm Nelda Reis. Is this your first time here?" She talked non-stop, calling a teenager over, introducing her to Christy and Timmy, and sending the teens off to their classes. As Nelda led Joe and me to our class, she told us how wonderful the church was, how wonderful the pastor was, how wonderful the Sunday School class was, how wonderful the teacher, Duane Brown, was, how wonderful the 150 people in the class were, how wonderful it is to be a Christian.

Finally, pausing for breath, she asked Joe, "And, sir, have you moved here on business?"

"Yes, we're assigned to this church to use the television equipment," Joe replied with a grin. "We're missionaries!"

Nelda's face changed from inquisitive to incredulous. Her eyes widened, as her smile bubbled over into laughter. "I don't believe it! I thought sure I had snagged an unchurched businessman and his family. I've been trying to convince you to become a Christian—and here you are, a missionary!" We joined her laughter and became instant, life-long friends.

Later, in the morning service, Jim Campbell, Associate Pastor, introduced us; and Pastor Strader welcomed us warmly. So did my old friend from West Florida youth camp days, David Thomas, Minister of Music.

We looked for a house to rent, but Tommy Dean Waldron (just a kid when we had worked for his dad in Beckley, West Virginia) had become a realtor and he convinced us we should invest in buying a house. He knew just the spot—a medium-priced area of town in a subdivision being developed by two men in the church. We looked at the new house: a split plan with two large bedrooms and a bath for the children on the left side. Living room, dining room, kitchen in the center. And on the right, the master bedroom, bath, and garage. There was even a large screened porch and a "Heatilator" fireplace in the living room. Perfect!

We stopped at furniture stores to ask if they had any slightly-damaged furniture. And we went to Sears' Scratch-and-Dent Warehouse where we found a huge, brown hide-a-bed sofa with soft cushions and just a small tear in the back. (Several years later, Timmy would take that monstrosity with him to a second floor apartment. Afterward, when he moved away from there, he tried to maneuver the old hide-a-bed back down the winding staircase. The sofa was so heavy and awkward, it gouged a hole in the wall, then another hole ... so ... Tim and his friend backed up and pitched the unwieldy monster off the balcony where it crashed and crumpled on the grass below!)

We were deeply thankful to have the transition year behind us. Both children said the year in Springfield was "the year from hell" because they felt so foreign and so dumb. They looked back on that year as "culture-shock-boot-camp," and they prepared to reinvent themselves into "North American teens" in Florida. They would not make the same embarrassing mistakes with these new kids at school and at church.

As far as I know, the term "Third Culture Kid" (TCK) had not yet been coined, but that is what missionary kids are: a third culture, neither wholly North American nor foreign. Rather, they are a blend. For the remainder of their lives. A TCK, unconsciously, observes body language; he listens for nuances of speech. His senses become heightened by adaptation, repeatedly, to different people, to changing situations, and to varying cultural norms. His worldview is different from that of his peers, and he tries desperately to "fit in." Some TCKs grow into brilliant, successful adults. Others flounder their entire lives. Parents learn that their missionary calling permanently affects their children. For better or for worse. Now, again, Christy and Timmy were forced to adapt.

Timmy, Margaret, Christy, Joe – 1978

Christy felt strange and uncomfortable at her new school, Kathleen High School. But she had learned a lot during the past year. To make friends, she joined drama clubs at school and at church. She loved John Taylor, the drama coach at church; he would become her mentor for years to come. She decided to change the spelling of her name; she would be *Crysti* now. Perhaps, it represented the "different-ness" she felt.

Timmy took his trombone, like a security blanket, to his new school, Kathleen Junior High School. He signed up for Beginner Band, but when the band director heard Timmy play, he promoted him to Advanced Band. Here, Timmy could "belong," could forge friendships, and have an identity.

Within a couple of weeks, Timmy played first chair in band and had found a cute girlfriend at church. He also joined a church drama group and attended junior high activities under the direction of a youth pastor chosen just for that age group: Randy Helms, a student at Southeastern College.

***

As we were moving into our new house, Joe received a phone call from Southeastern College. Their television production professor had resigned suddenly, and they needed Joe to teach the Television Production class. Joe accepted!

In those days, the college studio consisted of a small room with a low ceiling. It was located in a concrete block bungalow on the edge of the campus in a row of little old houses and former offices.

There were two old cameras, a switcher, a microphone, and a recorder for 3/4" videotape. The television director sat at the switcher to switch cameras, pushing button "one" or "two" to indicate which camera was "hot," (that is, being recorded onto the tape). The part of the switcher lying on the desk was about half the size of a cookie sheet. A lever could be moved backwards and forwards to "fade or dissolve" the shot from one camera to the other.

Joe was practically beside himself. He had equipment at his fingertips. He could produce something. Already!

He figured a sixty-second "spot" would be ideal for his very first production. It would be something similar to a Public Service Announcement (PSA) but telling the viewer about God. A Christian commercial. He would produce a series of such spots building from nature to the Bible to salvation in Jesus Christ.

Joe wrote the first script in Spanish. "*Dios creó* … God created beautiful nature for us to enjoy. He created the air for us to breathe, water for us to drink, delicious food for us to eat. God created animals to help us and to show unconditional love to us. But, [pause] why did God create *you*?"

In the tiny studio Joe recorded the audio, reading the script dramatically and adding music. The next step was to insert the video images. We searched for photos to illustrate each phrase. On poster boards, we mounted pictures to keep them from curling. We stood the posters on music stands in front of our two cameras. We would alternate cameras. Camera 1, images 1,3,5,7. Camera 2, images 2,4,6,8, etc. Joe would start the video recorder, playing the audio. Then he'd switch between cameras 1 and 2 as the audio indicated.

Our new friend, Eva, had already offered to help us, and she proved to be invaluable now and throughout the years to come. For this very first "spot," Eva and I would flip the pictures off onto the floor as soon as Joe switched to the other camera. But: we had not realized that each picture was a unique size and the camera had to be zoomed in and out and be re-focused every time. Joe's script went 'way too fast for us! Eva and I ran to flip the poster off, ran back to the camera, tried to refocus, missed the shot. Ran to flip.

Joe began hollering from the control room, "Take camera 1. Stand by 2. Take camera 2. Ladies! Hurry! What's taking you so long to line up the shot?!"

Finally, in total frustration, we realized the video would be absolutely atrocious because it depicted falling posters and women's arms and out-of-focus shots. We collapsed in laughter.

As the laughter died away, we comprehended the impossibility of ever accomplishing a "wonderful production." We could not do this! This ... our first project. A simple 60-second spot.

Totally frustrated, Joe stood up, ready to leave the little studio. He held the poster boards under one arm, the pitiful videotape recording in the other hand.

"Let's go to the church to see if Paul is there. Maybe he can salvage this mess," Joe sighed, with a deep, ragged breath.

A Place for People, Puppets, and Cockroach Soup

JESUS SAVES EVERYONE WHO ASKS.
JESUCRISTO SALVA A TODO EL QUE SE LO PIDE.

5

Paul

Here, let me help.

We drove to Main Street, where Joe parked our car alongside the church, next to the television production truck. Paul Garber hopped down out of the truck just as we approached.

Joe explained our dilemma and handed Paul the videotape. We climbed up into the truck, where an array of monitors, cables, and video machines enclosed us. Stacked floor to ceiling, metal shelves called "racks" held electronic equipment I had never imagined. Paul even spoke a foreign language, throwing out words like "TBC, CCU, quad, waveform, black level, gel, barn-doors, Par and Fresnel."

Paul sat at a desk-like area that resembled (to me) an airplane cockpit. He took our videotape and inserted it into one of his machines. Onto a monitor popped our footage. The first image was pretty good. But then chaos! Cards flipping at the wrong time, out of focus. Pathetic. Disgraceful. Actually, it was funny, but none of us was laughing.

Paul called out, "Greenlee, set up a camera!"

I watched in amazement. With a video-editor machine, Paul could pause the videotape. He could communicate with his cameraman, Rick Greenlee, on a headset. Rick could take his time focusing on the next picture. Rick knew which way to turn the handle to achieve the correct focus.

After a few minutes, Paul said, "We need something live—some video that moves. Let's see what we have on hand." He pulled a video he had shot at the Christian Retreat in Bradenton, Florida: a shimmering lake, colorful swaying plants, ducks paddling across the water. He inserted the footage. Beautiful!

When Paul finished, we held in our hands a beautiful, well-edited, Christian commercial. Our first, completed project—a Spanish spot by *STAR Productions*.

Many years later, Paul told us, "Even though the original spot was pitiful, the audio was good. And Joe's sincerity and desire to produce something meaningful shone through so strongly, that I wanted to help."

Joe cradled the tape in his arms while we walked across the parking lot to our new office. Another Paul—Paul Trimble—had approached us following the church service on Sunday night. "Do you have an office yet?" he asked. "I have a small building across from the church, on the corner of Main and Fern Streets. You can have office space. There's no charge."

We sat on the floor for several days, papers spread around us, just grateful to have an office. Adjacent to us was an empty room that we had persuaded Paul Trimble to "lend" to Tim's new youth pastor, Randy Helms.

A couple of days later, Joe went to Watson's Office Supply, a locally owned business, where we selected a desk, two chairs, and a file cabinet. As Mr. Watson totaled the bill. Joe said, "Mr. Watson, could you let us have this 'ninety days, same as cash'?" To our amazement, Mr. Watson agreed. Joe continued, "I have a missionary service Sunday in a church west of here. I'll tell them our need and see if they'll take an offering for us."

The following Monday, Joe walked into Mr. Watson's office with a check in hand. Mr. Watson shook his head, "I've never sold anything 'ninety days, same as cash' for only three days!" He stamped the bill "Paid in full." And from then on, anything we needed, Mr. Watson sold to us "ninety days, same as cash."

But now, Joe and I sat in our new office with the precious "first production" videotape on the desk. We decided to make two copies of this Christian commercial, our "spot." The first copy we would send to Guatemala to our old friends from language school, Dave and Mary Hansen.

Dave was thrilled. He took the tape to three TV stations (one with a nationwide audience). All three stations aired the spot for free. They loved it and asked for more.

We made the second copy for Eva to take to Puerto Rico to see if she could get it on the national channel there. She did. And surprisingly, a few weeks later, when she returned to Puerto Rico for a visit, she actually overheard some people talking in a restaurant at a nearby table. They were quoting phrases from the spot, using Joe's exact inflections, and saying how great it was to have a commercial honoring God. They said everyone they knew seemed to be talking about it.

The following spring, Joe entered the spot in a national contest sponsored by Evangel College. Amazingly, he came home with a big trophy—the spot won First Place!

That spot, the "first-fruits" of *STAR Productions*, began a ministry that we could never have imagined. It was as if Joe and I had begun to live in a different dimension in Lakeland. For the previous ten years, as missionaries in Chile and Paraguay, South America, we served far away from our donors. But by beginning this new ministry in the States, we lived side-by-side with our "enablers." We had always been interdependent, sharing the reward. Now the sharing became tangible. Joe and I continued to be "sent," financially dependent on missionary offerings. But now we would link arms, literally and physically, with people who for no financial gain, no recognition, and no play for power, simply and honestly gave of themselves to help us fulfill our ministry, our passion, our dream. Men and women who would sacrifice to help produce videos for people they would never see, who did not speak the same language, and who could never repay them. We would walk among saints (some more saintly than others, of course).

Over and over, God would bring to us the very people we needed at the very moment we needed them! Paul Garber, and others, took their places in this ongoing drama that was unfolding.

"I MAKE JOYFUL MUSIC TO MY LORD."
"CANTO CON GOZO A MI SEÑOR."

6

Juan

Nueva Vida (New Life)

October 1978

We produced several additional television spots, and then Joe wanted to produce a talk show. Relaxed format. Similar to what we'd produced in Paraguay. Lots of music. Conversation. We needed a host, a Latino, someone with a good sense of humor. Preferably, someone who could sing.

"Juan Romero" popped into our minds. We had met Juan in January, 1971, when we lived in Viña del Mar, Chile. Juan came to conduct a church revival in the neighboring city of Valparaíso. That night we walked into the church to hear the mariachi music (traditional Mexican street band) of Juan's music track. He wrote his own songs, ballad style, and loved the accompaniment of the loud mariachi trumpets and rhythmic guitars.

Being around Juan was both relaxing and refreshing. Juan grew up in Mexico and Texas, and his Spanish was excellent, his English not so great, but he was learning. We could jump back and forth from Spanish to English and laugh in both languages.

Joe called Juan on the phone, "*Hombre*, how would you like to host a TV show?" Juan was excited and also scared; he hadn't done anything like that before. But Joe assured him he would do great. We knew Juan was *real*, transparent, humble, anointed. Just the person we were looking for.

We coordinated a taping date with Paul Garber, who, with his crew, would shoot the show from the video production truck. Joe called Cypress Gardens—an outside shoot there would be beautiful! "Sure," they said, "just let us clear that with the *Back to the Bible* broadcast because they shoot here, too." In a few days, the answer came, "No. The other show will not agree to having another religious program shot in the park."

Deeply disappointed, Joe began to call various churches to find out if they had a fellowship hall with a high ceiling. We needed to set up tall poles for TV lights. And we needed a place to park the production truck.

Pastor Quentin Edwards, at Cypress Cathedral in Winter Haven, kindly agreed to let us use the fellowship hall there at no charge. Joe built some arches to serve as decorations, and found a rug and some suitable chairs. He called Shelton's Nursery, and Howard and Melanie delivered beautiful plants to decorate the set. (For years to come, the Sheltons would decorate our sets, totally free of charge.)

The *Nueva Vida* set

Joe could be on the set with Juan, to converse with him, but also we wanted a "guest," someone for Juan to interview. So, once again, Joe called an old friend we had met in Chile, Demetrio Montero Mendez, who was originally from the Dominican Republic.

Crysti and Timmy rehearsed singing in Spanish to music tracks, and Crysti practiced songs with her guitar. Joe prepared special music on his saxophone. I practiced singing, too. And of course,

Juan would sing all the other songs we would need to complete the formats. Altogether, we needed 39 or 40 songs to tape thirteen 30-minute shows.

We set up everything. Paul and his crew "lit the set," we decorated, and it was almost time to "roll tape." Then, Rick Greenlee, director, stepped out of the control truck and stated that there was no one designated to be "floor director." He asked me to do it. How? What exactly? I was petrified. Rick told me to relax. He would tell me what to say to the "talent"—Juan and Demetrio and Joe. I would wear a headset so that I could hear Rick's directions.

My voice shaking, I repeated what Rick said: "Stand by. Tape is rolling. 10, 9, 8, 7, 6, 5, 4..." I mouthed, "3, 2, 1." I motioned to Juan to begin. He did! We were taping!

As we neared the end of the show, I heard Rick say, in my ear, "Hold up the black wooden paddle with the number 5 on it. That will let Juan know there are 5 minutes left in the show." I did. "Hold up the 3." I did. "Hold up the 2." I did. "Hold up the 1, for one minute." I did. "Start moving your hand around in a circle to signal him to wrap it up. Hold up 10 fingers to indicate ten seconds, 9 fingers, 8, 7, 6, 5, 4, 3, 2, 1. Signal as though you're cutting your throat. Whisper 'Cut.' Good. Now tell them the floor's clear, that's a wrap. I'll roll the ending credits from the truck."

I said in a loud, nervous voice, "Clear. That's a wrap." I dropped to the floor, exhausted. Yet, I realized that I loved the adrenaline rush of being floor director. I had no idea, then, that I would be a floor director for the next twenty-six years!

That day we taped six 30-minute shows with the relaxed format of music and conversation. We called it *Nueva Vida* (*New Life*). It was good!

We had learned that television shows were usually shot in groups of thirteen because there are thirteen weeks in a television "season" of three months.

Joe continued to want to tape the rest of the series out-of-doors, so Paul arranged for us to tape at the Christian Retreat in Bradenton.

This outside shooting was complete with fluffy clouds, flowing palm trees, and ducks paddling in the pond. We won't mention the ants, the gnats, the mosquitoes, and the hot sunshine. As an alternative to recording only music, our new friend and helper, Eva, recited poetry in Spanish. She wore a long dress with flowing sleeves; she swept her arms dramatically, raised her face to look toward the heavens, and she spoke in artful, articulate accents that flowed from her lips.

Timmy and Crysti sang and then found ways to entertain themselves while the hours of shooting dragged on and on. Crysti hung out with Billy Register (no relation), another teenager whose dad, a pastor from Jacksonville, was speaking at the Retreat. She and Billy had fun telling people they were "Crysti and Billy Register."

Timmy happened onto a golf cart that had been parked near a path. The keys were in it, so he reasoned it must be available to anyone who needed to go from one place to another on the campus. Timmy hopped aboard and pushed the gas pedal. Whee! Away he went! He zoomed down paths, took corners as fast as the golf cart would go, slowed to pass old folks strolling along the lake. He stopped only when the battery ran down.

Later we discovered that the golf cart belonged to the founder of Christian Retreat, Gerald Derstine, and we understood why he was not happy that his cart had been "borrowed." Then, when we began to edit the music and poetry segments into the shows, we saw that something had been moving behind Eva. The object whooshed along a path ... it zipped behind Juan Romero ... it rocketed from left to right, then zoomed from right to left ... and finally, stopped dead. Was it a boy on a golf cart?

But, hopefully, no one else noticed the goings-on in the background. These shows were great—they were even better than the first of the series.

On November 13, 1978, Jim Campbell visited our mission headquarters in Missouri and took a tape of *Nueva Vida* with him. Subsequently, J. Philip Hogan, Executive Director, wrote to Joe, "I am happy to tell you that all of us on the committee ... were happily and gratefully surprised, not only at the format but the quality of the production. Surely these will be a start for us into some software that we have been desperately needing ... keep me informed of additional programs ... because I want to keep a little publicity going, especially in my personal appearances" (his personal speaking engagements to promote missions).

This letter was our first official approval. Not only had we shot our first shows, but we were now encouraged that *Spanish Television and Radio (STAR Productions)* would have a future. In only three months, the *dream* was becoming a *reality*.

In fact ... *Nueva Vida* was so good that Jim Bakker of the nationally televised PTL Club saw it and contacted Juan Romero to succeed Elmer Bueno as host of a Spanish PTL Club. We could not believe it! We couldn't hold Juan back from what appeared to be a much larger ministry ... but neither could we rejoice at our loss. Our talk show host was being pulled out from the heart of our show. We knew the Bible says that all things work together for good, but how could something *good* come from a loss like this when we were just getting started?

My heart ached. What on earth would we do now?

A Place for People, Puppets, and Cockroach Soup

JESUS SAYS, "You are my friends if you obey me." John 15:14 —TLB
CRISTO DICE: "Ustedes son mis amigos, si hacen lo que yo les mando." Juan 15:14—DHH

7

Bob

TV Channel 22 Clearwater, Florida

Spring 1979

I thought I would slide right down off the pew and dissolve into the carpet! How could the church do this? We had moved to Lakeland to use this equipment. My hands shook, my insides compressed against my spine.

About seven months after we had moved to Lakeland, on a Sunday morning as I sat in church alone (Joe was visiting another church to raise funds for our ministry), I heard pastor Karl Strader say, "We have just transferred all of our television equipment to Channel 22 in Clearwater, Florida, where Bob D'Andrea is beginning a new television station. Paul and all our crew are going there along with the equipment."

I knew the Bible says God prunes us to make us more fruitful, but this was no small pruning. God had not just snipped off a twig; He had gouged a huge hole in the trunk. We had lost Juan Romero, our TV host; and now, without the television equipment, we were totally stymied. Without Paul's help, we had moved to Lakeland in vain. We were *¡frito!* (finished!)

As soon as church dismissed, I called Joe. He was as calm as could be. "Don't worry. I'll talk to Paul when I get back. Something will work out. Don't panic!"

Paul was incredible. He told Joe that not only would he continue to help us but also he would not charge us a penny (we had been paying $1000 a day for the use of the equipment). What a blessing! Paul asked only that he be allowed to air our Spanish programming on Channel 22 for the Tampa Bay area—for free. Wow!

Later, Paul explained that in 1975, a group of pastors wanted to produce Christian programming to take advantage of the new "public access" policy on local cable television channels. That's when Pastor Strader, looking ahead, asked Paul to begin a TV production class at the church on Main Street. About 100 people attended the first class. When the students realized the focus would be work, not fun, only about ten people showed up for the second class. But from that class came the nucleus of Channel 22's crew: Rick Greenlee, Mark Greenlee, Carl Berger, Jan Brown, Wayne Elliott, Jim Gates, and Mike Stuckey. Most of these men literally quit their jobs to begin their work, by faith, at the new station.

Initially, Pastor Strader had wanted to build a television *station*. But even as Paul traveled to Washington D.C. to research all of the ramifications of obtaining a license to broadcast, Bill Register (the pastor in Jacksonville) came to meet with Karl Strader. Bill felt that a church should not be involved in building a TV station, because it would drain the church's resources and divert their attention. Besides, First Assembly already had a radio station (WCIE); plus the additional expenses of the TV production truck that was traveling all over the southeast to tape television programs for various ministries.

Pastors Karl and Bill talked at length. Karl acknowledged the amount of work and energy and money already being expended on radio and television productions by the Lakeland church. He realized that, when he began this project, he had no realistic concept of the enormity of the task of actually owning a *station*. But Bill knew a businessman, an electrician in Clearwater, Florida, Bob D'Andrea. He would probably help.

Bill arranged a meeting with Bob; Karl took with him to the meeting Jim Campbell (his associate pastor), and Paul. And what an electric encounter that was! For weeks prior to that meeting, as Bob would walk by a TV set, he felt God calling him to begin a Christian television station. But he knew nothing about television. He was an electrician. Now as Karl, Bill, Jim, and Paul shared their dream with

Bob, a burning desire flamed in Bob's heart. What if? Could he? God had blessed his electrical business. Was this why? Could it be so that he could help to develop a new, *Christian* television station for the Tampa Bay area?

Bob applied for a license to broadcast. Dr. Charles M. Leaming, founder of Florida Beacon College, donated part of his land. As soon as Bob received the construction permit, he hired Paul as General Manager and assigned him to design and build the station. Wayne Wetzel, a member of a newly formed "advisory board," donated some mobile homes to use as temporary offices. That is the point at which Pastor Strader traded the production truck, all of the video equipment, and his crew, for airtime on the new station.

In the spring of 1979, construction began. The *Christian Television Network* was born: Channel 22, WCLF, Clearwater, Florida.

Joe and I began to drive over to "the vacant lot with the trailers on it, Channel 22," every few days. The trip was about an hour each way, so we looked for housing in the area. When we told the realtor our price range, she looked at us with disgust. She took us to "the only thing you can afford"—a run-down house literally across the street from the city dump. Because housing in the coastal town of Clearwater was out of our price range—*way* out—we decided just to continue to drive back and forth from Lakeland. Besides, where we lived was not a high concern. The production truck would be able to meet us at various locations to shoot our shows because there was as yet no studio.

***

A few weeks later, Paul called Joe into his tiny office located in a trailer. "Joe, I want you and Margaret to produce a show in Spanish for children. I want Crysti, your daughter, to be hostess."

"Excuse me," Joe stammered. "We can't do that! We've never done shows for kids. Crysti is only sixteen years old. She can't host a show!"

Paul continued calmly, "Just produce one show. A pilot program. You can do it."

That evening Joe told Crysti about Paul's request. Astonished, she stuttered, "I can't do anything like that, especially in Spanish."

"Just pray about it tonight and let me know your decision in the morning. We'll have to start planning this 'pilot,'" Joe said and walked away.

The next morning Crysti agreed to "try."

8

John

What's the problem here?

A few friends sat with us around our dining room table to "brainstorm" ideas for the kids' television show—just one Spanish program, a "pilot."

Paul had said he wanted Crysti to host the show, but didn't she need someone to talk to? What would they talk about? What would be the setting? Should the set be imaginary? Realistic? My brain spun in my skull.

Then, Stephen Strader suggested, "Maybe the concept could be some sort of secret place for children, some imaginary place that Crysti could enter."

Ideas flowed: Maybe the secret place could be in her backyard. Maybe in a tree stump. Or be a hole in a big tree that would take her into the secret place.

The concept translated great into Spanish—we could call the show *El Lugar Secreto* (*The Secret Place*).

We would need a Bible story, a song, and an educational lesson of some sort. We determined that the format should be slow-paced, with a calming effect—similar to *Mr. Rogers' Neighborhood*. How would we open the show? How would we close it?

Who would Crysti talk to in this *Lugar Secreto*? Children? That would be a lot of work, to shoot when kids were not in school, to coordinate parents' schedules.

Suddenly, we remembered the four puppets stuffed in their box in Timmy's closet! Timmy dragged down the box and took out the man. He had a straight, black, shiny wig. A blue, turtleneck shirt covered his foam torso. No legs. Just an abrupt cut-off at the bottom of the shirt. Skinny brown arms dangled beneath the shirt sleeves.

Crysti reached for the woman. Her hair was longer and she had eyelashes glued to her plastic eyes.

We pulled out the girl. Ah, she was a little smaller, with long black braids, a pink shirt.

Timmy reached for the boy. He wore a striped shirt of bright colors. Timmy ran his hand up inside and turned the puppet's face toward his. They looked at each other for a long minute. Timmy said, "Hey, kid. You wanna be on TV? ... uh huh ... You wanna play the guitar? ... I'll bet you do, and I think your name should be, let's see ... *Beethoven*!"

(A few days later, Beethoven lay across Timmy's dresser, and Timmy, in a hurry, slammed the drawer on Beethoven's arm. I heard Timmy say, "Ayii, Beethoven, I'm sorry. I didn't mean to hurt you." Beethoven just stared back and didn't say a word.)

The day following our brainstorming meeting, we took the puppets and drove to "Main Street" (as we all called our church). We could practice in the old Pepsi building, which was now the church's youth hall. Joe put the man-puppet on his hand. He felt stupid. He didn't know how to open the mouth, how to make it talk, what to say. Timmy clutched Beethoven tightly, but had no idea what he should say. Crysti walked around looking lost.

Joe was doing such a bad job that I said, loudly, "That's terrible! I could do better with a puppet than you're doing." He handed me the puppet. I could NOT do better, and he let me know it! Joe growled at me. I snarled back. Crysti cried. Timmy and Beethoven cowered in the corner. We couldn't do it. We had failed. Utterly and totally. It seemed absolutely impossible to do a children's show.

After a few minutes of uncomfortable silence, Joe growled at Crysti, "Do you *still* want to *try* to do this!?"

"Yes," she whispered, a tear rolling down her cheek.

At that precise minute, a side door opened and John Taylor, the church drama director, walked into the room. John could feel the tension, could see our body language....

He grimaced, "What's the problem here?"

"John," Joe sighed, "we're supposed to produce a children's television show. We do *not* know how. We would like to work with puppets. But even if we knew how to operate the puppets and knew what to say, how on earth could we hide the puppeteers from the camera? We don't want the TV show to look like a children's church with puppet heads popping up from behind a curtain."

John thought for a moment, and then he said, "Joe, bring me that piano bench. Now, lie down, on your back. Slide under the bench until your head comes out on the other side. Raise your arms up on the back side of the bench."

Joe lay on the floor, under the bench. "Now, Crysti, sit here, on the end of the bench. Joe, where's your puppet? Put it on your arms, and hold them up, here, behind the bench. Crysti, turn sideways, and talk to the puppet."

Voila! A concept was born! A natural conversation flowed. The puppet "sat" on the bench beside Crysti. Joe's body was hidden underneath the piano bench. The camera could shoot from the top of the bench upward, avoiding Joe's body on the floor.

We hurried home, where Joe lay on the floor of the garage and asked me to measure from the floor to the top of his chest. It measured twelve inches. Joe would build a wooden platform twelve inches high that he could lie under. Crysti could sit on top of the platform—or, maybe, beside it?

And, oh, dear—what else would we need for this set?!

***

That is how John Taylor's life became intertwined with ours.

Which guy in the kiosk is John?

John, with his gentle, unassuming spirit, ignited a flame of creativity in Joe, Crysti, Timmy, and me that could not be extinguished.

Year after year, John would join us for productions as puppeteer, actor, and writer. His excellent Spanish served *Lugar Secreto* with humor and tenderness.

When puppeteers whom we could not even dream of—yet—would come to perform in our "shoots," John's love for Jesus touched their souls, and his incredible sense of humor kept us laughing hour after hour.

John Taylor would eventually become a missionary in Honduras, where he lives today. But during our years of producing *Lugar Secreto* and other productions, all we ever had to do was call, and John would come in a heartbeat to help us produce and shoot the next series.

9

Sue

That set looks pitiful.

Sue was our neighbor lady. One day, she looked out her window to see Joe lying on the floor of the garage, and then, the next day, she saw him building some sort of low, wooden platform. By the third day, she came walking over. Sue and Eldon Brown, missionaries to Asia, were home on furlough and had bought the house next door. In fact, Sue and Joe were first cousins; Joe's mom and Sue's dad were brother and sister, and the kids had grown up together.

Sue did not hesitate to tell Joe that his "set" looked really pitiful. With plywood, he had built a 3-foot by 4-foot wooden platform on legs twelve inches high. He tried to form a log of chicken wire on one end—so that when he raised his arms up from underneath the platform, his elbows would not be seen. He had given the log a branch, right in the middle. Sue said, "Joby, that branch looks terrible placed exactly in the center. If you would offset it a little, it would be more pleasing to the eye."

***

As our plans developed for the show, we decided to have Beethoven and some additional puppets perform the music segment. They could "sing" and "play" a song, miming to a cassette tape.

Joe searched for a tag inside the four puppets the woman from Oklahoma had given to us: H.O.P. Oklahoma City. What did H.O.P. stand for? *House of Puppetry*? What was that woman's name? It was unusual. *Fredda*. Fredda Marsh. Joe dialed "information" for her phone number. Could she help us? Could she send us one or two more puppets to help with music on the show?

Fredda shipped us a box. Free puppets. She even paid for the UPS shipping charge. We opened the box to stare at two of the most unusual things we had ever seen: a long-haired, green, bug-eyed frog puppet and his companion froggie-girl puppet. They had long, skinny, hairy, green arms and long, skinny, hairy, green legs. Yellowish blond wigs with fly-away fake shiny hair perched on top of their heads. The girl frog wore a flowered, sleeveless dress with a flared skirt. The boy frog's outfit looked like overalls, but with a flowered pattern. Their bug-eyes twisted freely, making them cross-eyed or wall-eyed from one minute to the next.

Fredda with Froggie Girl on her lap

By now, Sue was totally engrossed in what Joe was doing and decided to help him. Because our two "singers" were frogs, Joe and Sue decided to transform the platform into a pond. They could paint the surface blue, with some whitish shimmer. Sue added water lilies with leaves and flowers. She found a dragonfly and toadstools. The frog puppets could sit on the log (with the new off-set branch) and croak to their heart's content.

Now we needed an additional platform where Crysti could converse with Joe's puppet. Joe covered the second platform with grass carpeting and Sue spotted it with flowers. Joe made a stump from a wooden frame and covered it with chicken wire and burlap. Sue painted the stump various shades of brown. Crysti could sit beside the platform on the stump. Joe could lie underneath, holding his puppet up-top to talk with her.

To convey the idea of going into a *Lugar Secreto* (*Secret Place*), we still needed something for Crysti to enter. So Joe constructed a large hollowed-out space in a huge tree trunk ... made of chicken wire and burlap.

The plans developed further. When Crysti entered, she would find a puppet who lived there. In Latin culture, a person always greets everyone when he walks into a room. So as Crysti "came through the door" into the *Lugar Secreto,* she would look at the camera first of all to greet the boys and girls, welcoming them and drawing them into the *Lugar Secreto*. Then, Crysti would turn to the puppet and greet him with the usual Latino kiss on the cheek.

As we pictured this scenario, Joe decided we needed someone besides the "man puppet" to be the main character who would interact with Crysti. At this point, Joe went in search of the church's children's pastor, Shelby Lanier. Uncle Shelby took Joe into the puppet closet at church. Hanging behind the door was a yellow-orange monster-looking creature, drooped over a hook. He had a big mouth and lots of soft, fuzzy hair. "Could we borrow this guy for a few days?" Joe asked.

What could we call the yellow-orange fuzzy-one? Joe remembered laughing in Chile and Paraguay at a dumb joke Demetrio had told—about a dumb-dumb named "Bobo."

The name fit. *Bobo* would be soooooo dumb, and he would love to eat cockroaches and cook with them. His favorite song would be *La Cucaracha* (*The Cockroach*).

By this time, several more people were getting involved. David Thomas, the church's music director, volunteered to help. So did Christine (Chris) Miller, his fiancée. David rented a tux and played a piano solo. Chris, from underneath the "pond," operated a puppet-froggie "singer." Randy Helms' girlfriend, Karen, lay on the floor beside Chris and operated the other frog.

And so, on September 25, 1979 on the platform of the "Main Street" church in Lakeland, Florida, we "shot" our pilot show!

It was pitiful. *Bobo* sometimes forgot to open his mouth when he talked. Crysti was nervous; she stumbled on her Spanish words, and was hesitant to tell the Bible story with authority.

We showed the video to Paul. "Excellent!" he exclaimed. "Now produce a series of thirteen shows."

Many years later, we asked Paul why on earth he would say the program was good. He said, "It was good because you actually *did* it. Most people say they'll do something, they *want* to do something, but they never actually finish what they start. I knew you'd get better—if you had not improved," he laughed, "then I'd have stopped you!"

***

It had been obvious from the start that Joe did not know how to build a set or decorate one. So, when Sue Brown moved next door to us and then watched Joe struggle with his chicken wire log on our driveway, she knew that God had placed her next door to her cousin to help him.

Sue's companionship gave Joe confidence. Her artistic abilities brought beauty to the sets. And little did she realize that this was only the beginning for her. Many years later, *she* would produce children's shows in the country of Belgium in the French language, with the title: *Boulevarde des Enfants*.

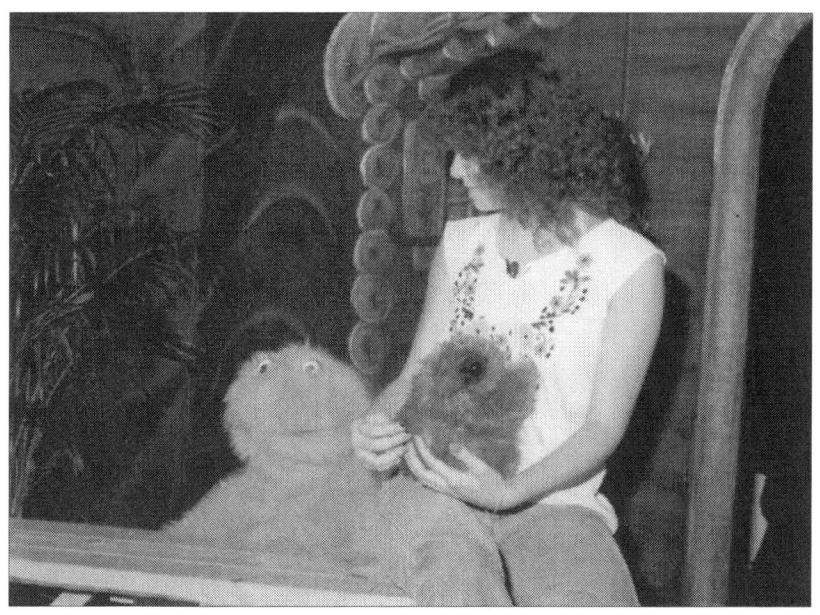

Bobo and "Cristina" on the first set
[Author's note: We still have our fuzzy, borrowed *Bobo*, thirty-two years later!]

A Place for People, Puppets, and Cockroach Soup

"REMEMBER FRIENDS, READ JOHN 3:16, "For God so loved..."
"AMIGUITO, NO OLVIDES LEER JUAN 3:16: "Porque de tal manera amó Dios al mundo..."

10

Cristina

I need help pleeeze.

1979 Continued

We were overwhelmed to think of producing thirteen Spanish children's programs. Talking about *Lugar Secreto* and about *Bobo* and *Cristina* (Crysti's television persona, her name in Spanish) became our daily bread.

The remainder of 1979 flew by. Joe traveled to the Dominican Republic to film a parade of Christians where thousands of youth marched through the streets on their way to the stadium for a victory rally. They carried banners proclaiming "Jesus is Lord." Pastor Waldron accompanied Joe—our dear, former pastor stood on the curb with tears streaming down his cheeks as he watched the parade. He had retired to Florida, but after this trip to the Dominican Republic, he said he could not just sit idly by, so he *un-retired*, and became the pastor of a small church in Lakeland. "Southside Assembly" was struggling at that time, but after several years, it became a vibrant, growing church and continues to this day.

That year, we also traveled to Mexico with the Waldrons and with Paul Garber to film educational segments with Monroe and Betty Jane Grams for our sister ministry *PACE (Program of Advanced Christian Education)*.

Throughout 1979 we distributed the series *Nueva Vida* to Guatemala, Puerto Rico, Peru, and Ecuador. We received a letter from Presbyter Victor Luna from Peru, "We began airing *Nueva Vida* in

May, and we are thrilled with the results. People are coming to our churches because of it."

We received a letter from Rubén Nieves, the Superintendent of Puerto Rico, "You cannot imagine how much help and blessing your television spots have been to us here."

Juan Romero invited us to Charlotte, North Carolina, to be on *Club PTL*, the Spanish PTL show. Joe and I, Crysti and Timmy each did music segments and interviews.

Tim and Crysti 1980
Singing in Spanish on *Club PTL*

Crysti with Juan Romero, *Club PTL*

In the meantime, I worked on themes for the series of *Lugar Secreto*. I found a small coloring book, *A-B-C-Dario Bíblico*, that we could use as a giveaway. We could even use the Bible story sequences for our themes. I searched for songs in Spanish and wrote opening and closing dialogues for Bobo and Cristina. I made a list of all the *props* (items to illustrate the theme) for each segment. And without realizing it, I became the producer of the shows.

Where could we shoot these thirteen shows? We needed to arrange our platforms, set up the lights, run cables for the microphones. We needed to organize the props in the order of the segments we would shoot. And, it was necessary to leave all this "set up" for about a week. The studio for Channel 22 was under construction in Clearwater, but not nearly ready yet. The production truck was parked there. Paul remembered that University Church of God in Tampa had a large choir rehearsal room where he had shot some videos for their pastor. Paul called the church and the pastor graciously agreed to let us shoot there.

As we recorded that first series, I realized that my hours of writing the dialogue between Cristina and Bobo had all been in vain. Their spontaneous interaction was much better, much more creative than anything I could write. So from then on, I just semi-scripted the opening and closing segments. Cristina and Bobo would get in place, in character, on the set. I would give them the theme for the first show, and then I would stand aside to watch their chemistry sparkle. As "Bobo" (Joe) and "Cristina" would begin to talk, ideas flowed out of their pores! When they were ready to "roll tape," we would record three minutes of joy and laughter and sometimes tears, but always with a clearly defined theme for that particular show. Bobo and Cristina did this time after time after time after time. It was beautiful to observe.

That first series was "OK." Not bad. Not great. Nevertheless, we made copies and sent them to missionaries in Guatemala, Ecuador, Puerto Rico, the Dominican Republic, Peru, and Colombia.

The missionaries were thrilled to have something for children and they asked for more. Station after station aired the shows "free," just grateful for wholesome, fun, kids' shows. In Colombia, David Lee began to show the videos in home patios, where crowds of children gathered to watch.

***

A letter dated October 12, 1979, arrived from the Division of Foreign Missions. We were officially approved. The probationary two-year-period was lifted after only fourteen months. *STAR Productions* could continue indefinitely!

***

Meanwhile, Crysti continued to struggle with the responsibility of "carrying the show" in Spanish. *Cristina* needed help. She begged us to find someone to help her on the set, especially someone to tell the Bible story.

***

Joe paced the floor. His heart raced. He marveled that his dream was becoming a reality! Now he must decide how to proceed. Gladly he had invited Juan Romero to be host of the talk-show. Juan took the lead; Joe was "side-kick." Now, in *Lugar Secreto*, Joe was behind and under the set. If this children's program became our flagship series, no one in Latin America would know Joe's name. He asked himself, "Am I willing not to be on camera? Am I willing to be behind the scene—literally?" No one would know that he was being a "good missionary," doing evangelism. No one would recognize him on the streets and say how wonderful the shows were. No one would know the hours of shoulder aches and headaches from operating a puppet. But God would. Was that enough?

Over a period of several days, Joe walked the floor, dying to self, praying. Then, he held up his head, called me over, and announced, "All right. It's all right that no one knows me. If we can reach children, and adults, through a 'silly' puppet show, through my being *Bobo*, then I yield to whatever God wants, however He wants to do this."

Joe wrote these words:

Jesus, You let them hurt You.
Then they nailed You to a tree.
Even the Father turned His back,
Just so Your love could reach me.

Use me, oh Lord, use me,
No matter what cost there might be.
If You need to step on me
to reach that soul,
Then use me, oh Lord, use me.

DIOS ME AMA A MI.

GOD LOVES ME.

DRAW A PICTURE OF YOURSELF HERE.
DIBUJA AQUI TU RETRATO.

11

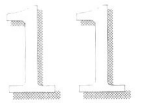

David T.

No speak-a de Spanish-a.

1980

"Mom, Dad! Can I go to Colombia? With a church group? They want me to sing in Spanish, and to be an interpreter!"

Crysti, a senior in high school, made sure her passport was current as she packed for two trips to Colombia that spring—both to Medellín. First, she traveled with the youth group, and then with *His Way*, a music ensemble of eight to ten voices directed by David Thomas. David had organized six different ensembles there on "Main Street" and many times they would average as many as twenty rehearsals a week.

David asked Joe, "Would you be able to teach *His Way* some songs in Spanish?" So, for several weeks, Joe worked with the group on phonetic memorization.

Two weeks prior to the trip, David Thomas and Christine Miller were united in marriage. And, of course, the ensemble teased them unmercifully, especially because Chris was sick part of the time in Medellín and couldn't leave the hotel.

Then, David was mugged! He was walking around the downtown plaza, as calm as could be, when suddenly two men bumped into him. In the "confusion," the thief lifted David's travelers' checks. He was carrying all of the ensemble's money—$400 in American Express travelers' checks and about $200 cash. David Lee, the missionary who had invited the group to Colombia, took David T. on a major cultural experience: a visit to the downtown police station to make a report of the incident. David Thomas was weak-kneed by the time the shouting and gesturing subsided. Thankfully, a short time later, being fully convinced of the robbery by proof of police documents and a nervous-wreck choral director, the American Express agent replaced the stolen checks.

Every night for a week in Medellín, *His Way* participated in evangelistic services. Crysti sang in Spanish, and her new friend, missionary Judy Bartel, preached. The services were held outdoors, right next to the soccer stadium, even competing with a soccer game on Sunday afternoon. To accompany the singing, David T. played a small keyboard with some of the keys missing. David Lee Jr. ran the audio and would shake his head in dismay every time David T. hit one of the "sour missing notes."

Crysti loved singing in Spanish, but *His Way's* phonetics began to wear thin after a few days, especially because so many of the State-side singers had deep, southern accents. The Colombians probably couldn't understand any of the words by the end of the week, but they could see the joy on the singers' gringo faces.

When the group returned, the newlyweds brought back a new set of dishes and some of the stolen-recovered expense money, which David divided among the singers to help with their expenses.

And, wonder of wonders, Crysti brought back news of her very special discovery: someone who could tell the Bible story on *Lugar Secreto*—her new friend, Judy Bartel. Judy had grown up in Colombia where her parents, Harry and Martha Bartel, served as missionaries. Judy's Spanish was practically flawless, and her gentle spirit and quick smile had endeared her to Crysti.

Returning from Colombia, Crysti had no more than bounded in the door, when she began to plead, "Daddy, please call my new friend, Judy. She is wonderful. Perfect for the Bible story. Here is her phone number. I've told her all about *Lugar Secreto*. Please, please, pleeease call her."

Joe did. And Judy agreed to come. She had only one request, "May I bring two young ladies with me? They are good puppeteers, taught by missionary Linda Stewart. The young ladies are sisters; their names are Maritza and Sara (Sarita) Segura. I'll try to find a sponsor to pay their way."

***

David Thomas' simple decision to take his music group to Colombia would eventually change the lives of tens of thousands of people. What if he had refused to go?—after all, it was actually his honeymoon! If he had not obeyed God in this simple act of obedience, would he have been invited by Pastor Dan Betzer to move to Fort Myers, Florida? To be named Minister of Music at First Assembly of God, and then become the Senior Assistant Pastor to thousands of people?

And, as for *Lugar Secreto*, would we ever have known that three multi-talented and dedicated women named Judy and Maritza and Sara had been predestined by God to become an integral part of *STAR Productions*?

A Place for People, Puppets, and Cockroach Soup

JUDY SAYS, "GOD THINKS YOU ARE SPECIAL!"
JUDY DICE: "¡DIOS CREE QUE ERES ESPECIAL!"

12

Maritza and Sarita

We're scared to death!

Summer 1980

Government agents with dogs threaded through the huge holding area on the never-ending search for drugs. Sarita heaved her heavy suitcase up onto the counter. Maritza pushed her luggage up onto the metal counter, too. The women's hands shook from fear of the customs inspector.

Maritza and Sarita Segura, traveling out of Colombia for the very first time, stood in a long queue in the Miami airport as they waited for their new passports to be stamped. At least the agents spoke Spanish! Judy ushered the young women to the luggage pick-up carousel, and from there the three women had maneuvered their suitcases over to the customs inspections' long, low tables. Sarita worried about the small puppets she had "hidden" in her luggage; Maritza worried about the props she had packed, things very unusual to be in a suitcase.

The inspector rummaged through the suitcases, and at last she said, "Okay. You're cleared." She waved the women off, gestured to the line of people waiting. "Next?!" she shouted.

Judy found a cart for all the luggage and led the way back upstairs to find the connecting flight to Tampa. Maritza and Sarita were scared—scared they would not do a good job "for TV." They had operated puppets for Colombian kids but not for thousands of television viewers. Myrna Wilkins, a missionary in Colombia, had paid their way to make this trip. Would they disappoint her?

Joe and Crysti met the young women at the Tampa airport and drove them to Bethel Temple (now Bethel Church) on Hillsborough Avenue in Tampa. Pastor Gordon Matheny had offered the opportunity for the women to stay in the little cottage at the back of the church property.

The next day we met at Channel 22, in Studio C. Although far from completion, the station had much of the drywall in place, and we would not interfere with construction if we stayed back in our little corner of the building. Joe flung open the big overhead doors so that we could get some fresh air and adequate light.

I had talked to Judy on the phone regarding the themes for these thirteen shows, our second series. Judy said that Sarita was really good at writing scripts for short dramas for puppets. Maritza could edit the scripts and also fabricate and collect props for each drama. Also, Judy said the two women could record the thirteen dramas there in Colombia and bring the audio tapes with them.

So on our first day of rehearsal, as we gathered in the unfinished room, Joe put the tape in the machine and the audio began playing. But Sarita and Maritza just clutched their puppets to their chests and stared at us. Where was the puppet stage with the PVC pipes and the long curtains? Where could Maritza and Sarita hide? There was no way they could "do a puppet show" unless they hid behind something. Sighing, Joe pulled a piece of plywood over, propped it up, and the women sat down on the concrete floor behind it. Joe started the audio tape again.

The puppets popped up from behind the board. Sarita waited to hear her puppet's voice and then began to move her puppet's mouth. Maritza did the same.

"No! Wait!" Joe exclaimed. "We can't do it like this—like children's church. The voice and mouth movements have to be perfectly synchronized. You'll have to read the script 'live.' Do you have your script there?"

"*Si-ii* (Ye-ess)," they said timidly.

"All right. Begin from the top. First puppet speak," said Joe.

Silence.

"*¿En vivo?* (Live?)" whispered Sarita.

"*No podemos* (We can't)," quavered Maritza.

"Sure you can. You have to," Joe said. "We have to have real-time mouth movement. It cannot be delayed while you are waiting to hear the audiotape-timing."

Sarita looked ready to burst into tears. "*No puedo* (I cannot)."

"*Imposible*," echoed Maritza, sadly.

We broke for the day. Judy, Maritza, Sarita, and Crysti went back to the little cottage behind the church. When they opened the door, a roach went flying across the room!

"I want to go home," sobbed Sarita. "I cannot operate a puppet *live*. This—this Florida—it is too hot, too humid, and there are too many bugs."

The four young women sat in a circle on the bed. They clasped hands, and Judy prayed. Then Judy said, "You don't have to stay. You don't have to do this. But think what a tremendous opportunity this is! Perhaps, tomorrow, you could just *try*."

The next morning a very pale Sarita walked slowly into Studio C. A pale Maritza followed her. They held up their puppets; they took a deep breath, and weak, little puppet voices wavered through the first words. The second sentence sounded ever-so-slightly stronger. The third better. They finished the drama. We applauded! They did it! They could do it!

We rehearsed all thirteen dramas. Judy operated some characters; so did Crysti and Timmy and Joe. One of the dramas included various animals talking. Sarita, comfortable now in handing out scripts and assigning roles, handed me a little lion puppet she had brought from Colombia. We began to rehearse our lines.

"Ro-ar," said the lion on cue, as I opened my lion's mouth and said the word "roar." Joe catted his eyes at me. Judy grinned. Sarita frowned. Maritza smoothed her script.

"*Otra vez* (Again)," called Sarita.

"Ro-ar," my lion said.

"Margaret, do it right. Quit playing around," Joe ordered.

"I am!" I told him sincerely.

Joe reached over, took the puppet off my hand, and handed it to Timmy. "Margaret, you can just help with the props," Joe said with a grimace and a grin. Everyone laughed out loud.

They don't let me operate a puppet to this day!

***

I was amazed at the quality of these scripts. The writing was really good. Sarita could "turn a phrase" in Spanish—artfully employing puns, twisting phrases for humor, and then before you knew it, punching-in the moral of the story.

***

Weeks before, as we made our "pre-production" plans, we knew we needed better sets and our own "flats" for this, our second series. To shoot the pilot and the first series, we had borrowed, from Uncle Shelby's children's church supplies, a flat to stand behind Bobo and Cristina. Now, Joe and Sue designed 4-foot by 8-foot lightweight, wooden frames. Local fabric stores sold burlap, but we needed yards and yards of it, preferably of the natural, tan color so that we could paint it to our specifications. After many phone calls, Joe located a company in Louisiana that sold burlap by the roll.

Once again, Joe had converted our garage and driveway into a construction zone. He fashioned the wooden frames, stretching the burlap tightly on them.

Sue in her living room

Sue's living room had a cathedral ceiling, twelve feet high ... and Eldon, her husband, was gone for several weeks ... so she put down a drop cloth to keep paint off the carpet. Banana trees, vines, and tall trees with drooping branches began to take shape in Sue's living room. By the time Eldon returned, the beautiful flats had been removed and the spilled paint cleaned up. The stretched carpet was more or less restored to normal. We still don't understand how he noticed that something had been going on in his absence....

Joe called Fredda again, "We've been asked to produce thirteen more shows. Would you be able to send us some more puppets?"

"Sure. How many do you need? Human or animal?"

"Both. And legs. Do you have any puppet legs? ... Yes, I know they're heavy for the puppeteer to hold in the air, but we are showing the entire 'body.' Can you fasten the legs to the torso with Velcro?"

Joe began to design the set for this series. For an opening and closing set, he designed a "flat" with a door. Cristina could come through the door into the *Lugar Secreto* where Bobo would be waiting for her under his platform.

For the music segment Joe designed a hillside for the puppets to sit on. The Froggies could sing, Beethoven could strum his guitar, and any new puppets could also be sitting there whatever their genre, human or animal. Joe built a wooden frame, slanted up. He formed the bumpy hillside with chicken wire. He cut out "holes" for the puppeteers' arms to come through; he bent the wires back snuggly so the puppeteers underneath the set would not get scratched (much). He covered the hillside with burlap, saturating the cloth with "sizing" to keep it stiff. Then he and Sue painted the new set with varying shades of greens and browns.

By being slanted, the hillside provided places for puppeteers to lie down, kneel, or sit on a stool underneath. We would place the puppets on top, so that the puppeteers (from underneath) could run their arms up into the puppet. Joe rented a truck to haul the large hillside and the flats from our house to the studio.

***

Finally, the day arrived for our first rehearsal of the music segments. We set up in Studio C; then we tried to accommodate each puppeteer according to the height of that puppet's hillside hole: a blanket to lie on, a pillow to kneel on, a stool or folding chair to sit on. I, not being able to operate a puppet (smile), would become the "floor director" and would try to see that the puppets' legs were straight and their clothes neatly arranged.

Joe, Timmy, Crysti, Judy, Sarita, Maritza—all were tucked up under the set, each person in a varying degree of discomfort! I pressed the button for a music tape to begin. (We could use a tape for music because the rhythm gave a definite cadence for puppeteers to follow. The music made timing the mouth movements easy.)

The puppets began to sway and sing; Beethoven strummed his little guitar.

Suddenly, out of the corner of my eye, I saw something slither in through the big overhead doorway. A snake! Escaping from the swamp just outside, the unwelcome visitor had found some shade and a cool concrete floor. Decision. It had taken *forever* to place the puppeteers. If I yelled, "Snake!" they would knock over the set! They would scrape themselves on the chicken wire!

"Better to wait until the song ends," I thought. "Then I'll tell them to 'take a break.'"

I held my breath. The song finally ended. I pushed the stop button. I said calmly, "OK, guys, great job! Now, let's get out from under there for a break. Careful. Don't scratch yourself. Come on, everybody out."

Bent backs, aching bodies crawled slowly out from under the hillside set. When everyone was in sight, I said, "Uh. Maybe we should go out into the hallway. During that song… a snake crawled in here—"

Screaming loudly, "*Ayii, no. ¡Vamos!*" Everyone scrambled for the doorway.

***

Because the studio was under construction, we could rehearse but not shoot there—so we needed a place to "film" this series. Joe called Don Lunsford, the new pastor at Clearwater First Assembly. "Don, does your church have double doors? It does? Could we shoot a series of children's TV shows there? The music set I built is so big, it only fits through double doors." Pastor Don readily agreed and even let us leave the sets on the church platform during his Wednesday night service.

In talking with Rick Greenlee, the Channel 22 director assigned to the truck, we decided to shoot all thirteen music segments first.

Then we would tear down that set, and arrange the stage for the thirteen dramas. After that, we would shoot all the openings, followed by all the Bible stories, and so forth.

Early one Monday morning, we drove the rental truck to the church and unloaded our sets and flats and puppets and props. The Channel 22 production truck pulled up outside and began to set up tall light poles and run cables for lights and microphones.

Soon after the production truck arrived, the production crew sat waiting—signaling with voice and body language, "Let's go! What are we waiting for now? Let's shoot!"

The pressure on Maritza, Sarita, and me was heavy—we needed to have every prop, every puppet, every script organized for every segment. We arranged the props in order of use, laying them on the church pews. The most challenging part was organizing everything for the thirteen dramas with their numerous characters, costumes, and distinctive props. We would need to shoot the dramas out of sequence, utilizing each unique set two or three times. When the shows were edited, dramas from the same set would be scattered throughout the series.

We did fine! Fine, that is, until the middle of a puppet drama about the little beggar boy who learns he is actually a prince. The trumpet sounds and the little *gamín* (beggar boy) stands before the king, who places the royal crown on his little head. That is to say, the king is *supposed to place the crown* on his little head.

However, the king puppet was a "human hand" puppet, meaning that two people had to operate him. One person operated the head; another person operated both of the arms (which were "real arms" inside the puppet's shirt sleeves, with real hands extending into puppet gloves). The "hands" puppeteer had to stand behind the "head" puppeteer and reach around in front of both the "head" puppeteer *and* the puppet's foam body.

Sarita, the "hands" puppeteer, held the crown. Maritza operated the king's "head and body." Sarita raised the crown ready to bring it down on top of the beggar's head—but where was his head? Sarita could not see around Maritza.

Judy operated the beggar boy. He awaited his crown.

The king (Maritza, in a deep voice) said, "I now crown you ... ah ... I now crown ... you...."

The crown wavered up and down, slid side to side searching for a head to land on.

The king repeated, "And now I crown you… uh…"

Judy peeked around her beggar boy puppet. She could see the crown swaying back and forth and up and down. She dipped the beggar's head; she raised his head; she tilted it from side to side trying to follow Sarita's movements. When the beggar zigged, the crown zagged.

The king repeated frantically, "I hereby crown you…."

Finally, in desperation, Judy jammed the beggar's head up under the crown. Sarita's hands released it. The crown tilted precariously, down over one little, plastic, beggar's eye. The eye popped off and rolled to the floor.

Quickly, Judy exclaimed, "I am a prince!"

The director yelled, "Cut! That's a take!"

We collapsed onto the floor in gales of laughter. The cameraman, Mark Greenlee, flopped down from his camera to lie on a church pew. He rolled with laughter as tears flowed down his cheeks. Although he could not understand the Spanish language, he certainly saw what happened—on *his* camera shot!

The next day, we tore down those sets and set up the Bible story set for Judy. Among the puppets from Fredda were a little boy and a little girl. Maritza took the little boy who was dressed in blue; she named him *Tomasito*. Sarita took the little girl in the red velvet dress. She named her *Rosita*. Tomasito and Rosita sat beside Judy as she told the Bible story. She talked to them and to the viewer. Tomasito and Rosita asked questions. The interaction was great. Judy was wonderful! So were Tomasito and Rosita.

Then we tore down that set and set up the "home set" where we would shoot the openings and closings with Bobo and Cristina. We shot all thirteen openings. Then, for the closings, Rosita and Tomasito joined Bobo and Cristina. They all sang as Cristina played her guitar. They would sing an extra long time, so that we would not have to worry about the length of the show. When the segments were edited together, we needed exactly 28:50 (28 minutes and 50 seconds) per thirty-minute show.

Exhausted, yet joyful, our new, small, valiant cast and crew had succeeded in shooting segment after segment. In spite of challenges, on our limited resources, through laughter and through tears, we had produced the second series of *Lugar Secreto*.

Although we did not have expertise as puppeteers, and although we certainly were not professional set builders or professional script writers, yet we were motivated by a desire to serve God with all our hearts. At one point during these weeks, we read this quote from George Washington Carver:

"Do what you can, with what you've got, and do it now."

Wow! What a brilliant saying—it struck a responsive chord in our hearts and became our motto. Don't wait. Don't wait until you know how. Don't wait until you have all the resources you need. Don't wait until the circumstances are perfect … just do what you can with what you have … and do it *now*.

"Now" all we needed to do was to edit these shows, duplicate tapes to send to television stations and missionaries, and, oh, yes, pre-produce the next series.

**

Very few people are as precious to me as Maritza and Sarita Segura, who gave up their personal lives in order to become script writers, puppeteers, administrative assistants, and actors with STAR.

In their complete dedication to reaching children with the Good News of Jesus Christ, they forfeited financial gain and ignored personal recognition. Sarita wrote scripts, enhanced by Maritza's editing skills. Maritza authored the *Lugar Secreto Teacher's Guide.* She translated numerous adult Bible study lessons that Sarita polished with her unique word skills. In so doing, Maritza and Sarita became spiritual mothers and sisters to children, youth, and adults from the southern tip of Argentina to the northern reaches of Canada, from New York to California, and then west and east around the world.

From their native Colombia and from *STAR,* Maritza and Sarita continue to "shine like stars in the universe as they hold out the word of life." (Philippians 2:15-16, my paraphrase)

Sarita and Maritza Segura with *Rosita andTomasito*

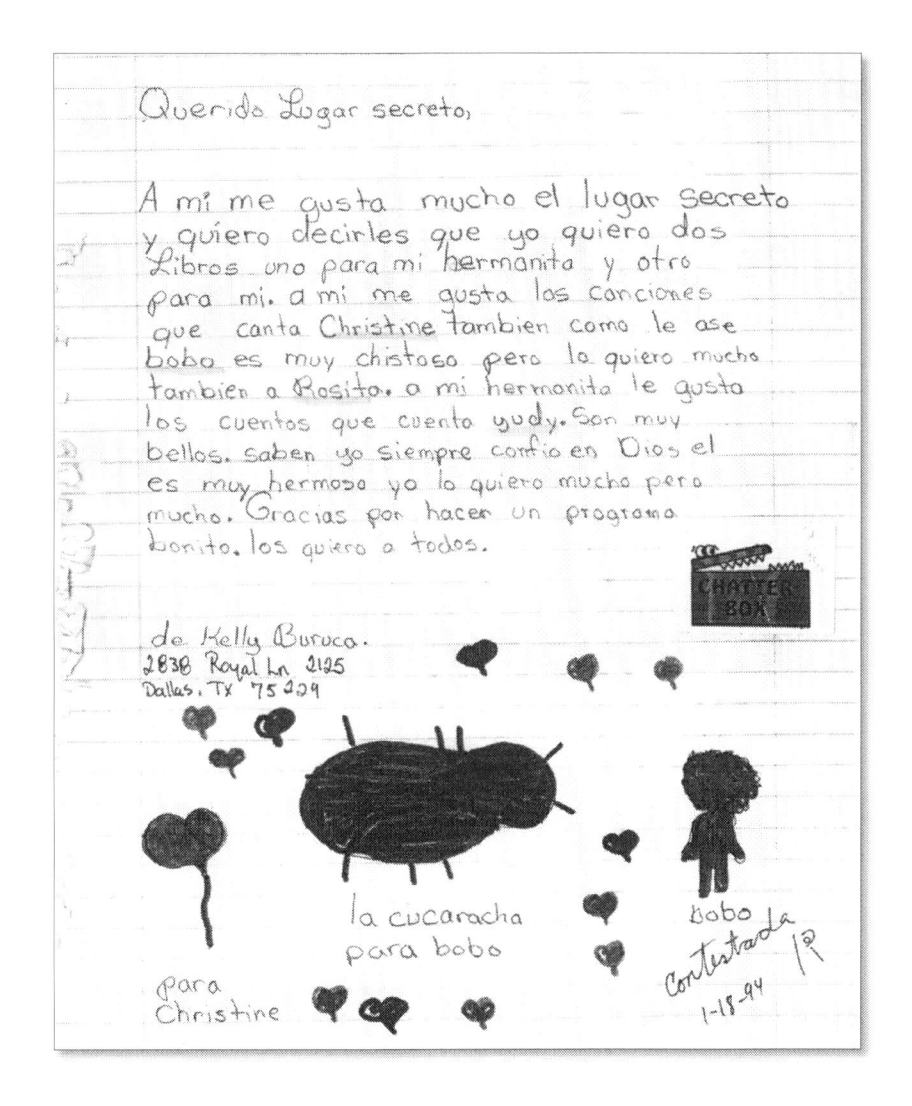

> Querido Lugar secreto,
>
> A mí me gusta mucho el lugar secreto y quiero decirles que yo quiero dos Libros uno para mi hermanita y otro para mi. a mi me gusta los canciones que canta Christine tambien como le ase bobo es muy chistoso pero lo quiero mucho tambien a Rosita. a mi hermanita le gusta los cuentos que cuenta judy. Son muy bellos. saben yo siempre confio en Dios el es muy hermoso yo lo quiero mucho pero mucho. Gracias por hacer un programa bonito. los quiero a todos.
>
> de Kelly Buroca.
> 2838 Royal Ln 2125
> Dallas, TX 75229
>
> la cucaracha para bobo
> para Christine
> bobo
> Contestada
> 1-18-94

"Dear *Lugar Secreto*, I really like *Lugar Secreto* and I want to tell you that I want two books, one for my little sister and one for me. I like the songs Cristina sings and also how Bobo is. He is very funny. Also, I like Rosita very much. My sister likes the stories that Judy tells. They are great. You know, I trust in God. He is wonderful and I love him a lot, a really lot. Thanks for doing the great programs. I love you all. Kelly"

A Place for People, Puppets, and Cockroach Soup

CAPTAIN ALAN AND HIS FRIENDS WELCOME YOU TOO.
EL CAPITAN ALAN Y SUS AMIGOS TE DAN TAMBIEN LA BIENVENIDA.

13

David L.

Is video a valid ministry tool?

1981

As 1980 drew to a close, we felt overwhelmed. Everything in our world screamed, "PRIORITY!"

We *had* to raise funds. We needed to buy wood and paint and nails and fabric for sets. We needed to purchase props and videotapes, pay postage to mail copies to other countries, and obtain office supplies.

We *had* to call pastors and schedule services to tell the congregations about what we were doing at *STAR Productions*—and what we wanted to do, with their help.

Joe *had* to travel to churches to conduct the scheduled services and then receive an offering.

We *had* to finish editing the second series of *Lugar Secreto*. We possessed hours of "raw footage," hours of the ninety-one segments shot (many of them with "take 1," "take 2," meaning that specific segments had to be selected before they could be edited into shows). I had to list each segment's location: Program 15, Opening on tape 23, cut 4; Music on tape 25, cut 3; Drama on tape … Bible story on tape …. Once I had the list ready, we needed to schedule time in the TV production truck to edit these shows. Linear editing, it was called. There was nothing digital, no computers, nothing except a long plastic line of audiotape or videotape or a combination of both.

Letters of requests piled up on the desk. "Please send us the next series. We are showing re-runs." This back-log of orders came from

Bridgeport, Connecticut and from Puerto Rico, Costa Rica, and three cities in Perú; from Panamá, Guatemala, Ecuador, Bolivia, and Colombia. Also, missionaries in Argentina, Paraguay, and Uruguay, were waiting for tapes to be converted to their video system.

But before we could send copies of thirteen new shows, we *had* to duplicate the edited shows. Duplication was in "real time." That is, a thirty-minute show took thirty minutes to copy. But before we could copy it, the virgin videotape had to be "formatted"—run through the machine with color bars and audio tone. This took one hour per tape. So, to copy a series of thirteen shows for one country, we spent a minimum of fourteen hours just making the copies.

We were paying to have a "character generator" add the local address to every tape, so that viewers could write in to a local missionary for the giveaway and for follow-up. But, if we could build a small room in half of our garage, we could purchase our own character generator (an electronic typewriter that typed letters on the screen and then transferred them onto the videotape). With two videotape machines connected to the CG (character generator), we could do this ourselves. Of course, we *had* to raise the money for that. Then we actually had to construct the room and purchase the lumber and drywall and carpeting for the walls. In addition, we needed to build a sturdy desk-counter and run electricity to the room.

Also, we *had* to begin the pre-production for the next series. Sarita needed themes so that she could begin to write the dramas. We needed to find and schedule a locale to shoot the series, and schedule the production truck.

Our boat was sinking. We were overwhelmed mentally and emotionally and physically. *Had-to's* screamed at us, even in our sleep. We had progressed from 0 to 100 miles per hour in two years!

Our family suffered. Yes, Crysti received her driver's license; yes, she and Timmy spent many after-school hours at the church in youth and drama activities. And yes, they loved listening to the church's contemporary music on WCIE. But, sadly, during their high school years, Joe and I did not spend the personal family time with them that we should have; in fact, we didn't even put up a Christmas tree that year—we felt we "didn't have time."

A Place for People, Puppets, and Cockroach Soup

Joe in the garage "suite"

Where could we find help? We had no funds to pay anyone a salary. Volunteers were wonderful, but their time was limited. We needed someone who spoke Spanish, who had some technical expertise, who could work full-time. And most importantly, someone who *believed in* what we were doing.

The concept of using media was new to Christianity. In many people's minds there was no place for "television shows" in church work. And many thought that, certainly, there was no place for puppets, of all the ridiculous things, in ministry.

But we knew a missionary who believed in the media; in fact, he was using radio and television where he lived and ministered. He believed in ministry to children, too. Joe called David Lee in Medellín, Colombia. David was reluctant to leave the foreign field and return to be stationed in the U.S., but for him the possibilities of ministry through the potential outreach of *STAR Productions* overrode any other concerns.

In early 1981, David and Jimmie Ruth Lee, along with their children, David Jr. (Davy), Stephen (Stevie), and Cindy (who was actually already away at nursing school), joined us at *STAR*. We had no building, and the previous, borrowed office space was located in the opposite direction from Channel 22, so David bought a house with a garage, which he then converted into a double office.

Editing and duplicating take time. And we had imposed on the good will of Channel 22 for hundreds of hours. We needed our own equipment. We talked about a crazy idea: What if Channel 22 bought another, smaller, production truck? What if we could find funds for the video equipment to furnish the truck?

Paul asked Bob. "Yes! Channel 22 will buy a truck."

We asked our Foreign Missions leadership. "Yes! We will commit for the equipment." Fortunately, the Assemblies of God has a wonderful way to help youth participate in missions. Every church youth group is challenged to set an annual goal—to wash cars, bake cookies, ride bikes in marathons—anything to raise money for missions. They call it *Speed-the-Light* (STL), and most of the funds are designated for vehicles, but evangelism "tools" also receive aid. All the monies raised are sent to "headquarters" and held in a special account. Missionaries petition the Foreign Missions Committee for a disbursement. Now, after our needs were presented to them, STL allocated $150,000 for our video equipment!

The 14-foot Ford box-truck became our remote control room and editing suite. But because duplication takes many hundreds of hours, we relied on the two old videotape machines in the little room inside our garage, as our "duplication department."

A few days after the Lees arrived, we set up the cameras in our back yard so Jimmie Ruth and David Jr. (Davy) could practice running camera. Within minutes, Davy could zoom and pan and tilt and focus like the pro he would become.

***

We held our production that summer in the Southeastern College chapel. Joining with our two families was a new guy, Alan Skogerbo, a student at Evangel College. When Joe earlier had spoken at a video seminar there, Alan approached him, "Say, could you use any help? I'm an MK (missionary kid), speak Spanish fluently, and am a magician, a carpenter, and a puppeteer." Alan soon became *El Capitán* (Captain Alan), a regular on the shows, and would become producer of the shows in English.

A Place for People, Puppets, and Cockroach Soup

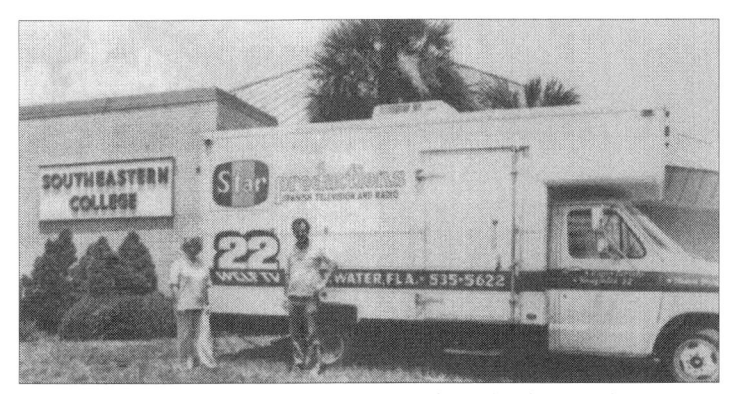

David and Jimmie Ruth Lee beside the truck

That month of production was our best to date—and one reason was a new concept of set design. Several months earlier, Paul Garber handed Joe a videotape of a Muppet show. It was the John Denver Christmas Special. The Muppets, of course, set the standard high for puppeteers, and they closely guarded their secrets. Their studio was closed to all visitors, and no one knew how the Muppets could move about so freely, literally turning around, and walking *everywhere*.

In the little room in our garage, Joe watched the video. He watched it again. He watched it again. And again. And again. Suddenly, Joe noticed that when John Denver entered the Muppets' dining room, he glanced to the side and downward. Joe paused the tape. Rewound it. Watched it again. Hmm. Why does John Denver not just walk confidently into the dining room? Why does he glance *down*? Could it be because he was conscious of where he stepped? Cautious, even?

Joe breathed a prayer. He watched the sequence again. And again. All at once, ¡*voilá, gestalt*! Joe realized that John Denver was not walking on the floor. The real floor. He must be on a ramp, above the floor. That meant … the puppet operators were walking on the real floor.

There must be a second, higher, imaginary, suspended floor … Hmm. If a puppeteer held his puppet straight up in the air, and if the puppet's feet came to about waist high on the puppeteer … and if you built a small platform about waist high … and you placed a puppet-sized dining room table on the platform … the puppeteer could walk up to the table, puppet aloft … but a real-person-actor (like John Denver) would need to be elevated up off the real floor, so that his body would be proportionate to the pretend-floor-platform where the puppets lived.

Timmy on set, waiting, leaning on "platform,"
A "flat" Sue painted is behind him.

This concept was revolutionary! And the Muppets did not reveal their secret for another decade. When they did and we looked at their platforms, we discovered that ours were identical. For Joe went straight to the other half of the garage and began to design wooden platforms two-feet wide, four-feet long, and three-feet high. He hinged the sides for easy storage; he made the top of 3/4" plywood, sturdy enough for a person to walk on. On the platform, we would place tables, chairs, beds, sofas—everything a puppet needed in his world three feet above the real floor. We cut holes in the backs of the chairs for the puppeteers' arms. We built sofas and little beds, and occasionally we bought used, children's furniture.

***

Sarita's scripts were better than ever. New puppet personalities, created by Sarita's witty pen, emerged, flourished, and became "regulars" on the show.

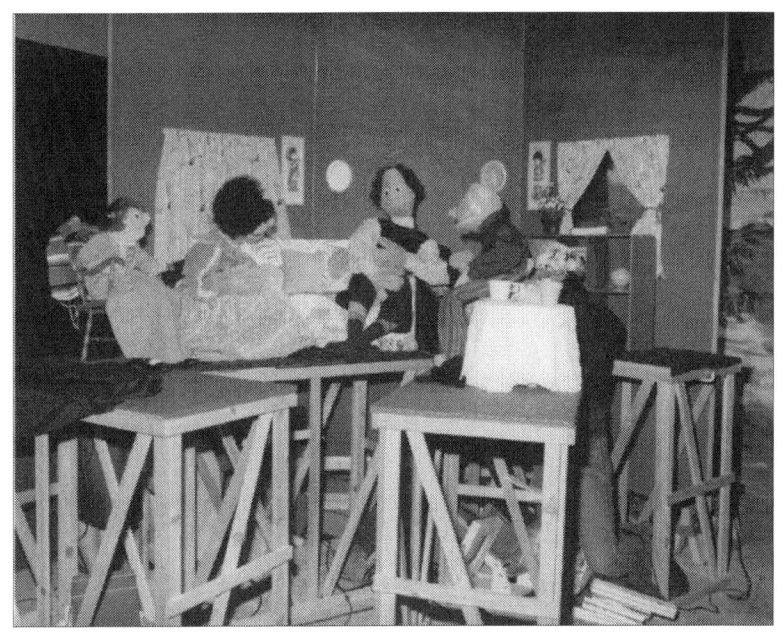

A living room scene

The year 1981 flew by! And before we knew it, the Foreign Missions Committee asked David and Jimmie Ruth Lee to move to Brussels, Belgium, to begin a television ministry there. David called it *International Media Ministries* (IMM).

***

Although David joined us for only a few months, he brought credibility and open doors for fund raising for *STAR*. He had served as Youth Director of the Peninsular Florida District, and he knew every pastor in Florida. When he became a missionary in Colombia, South America, he never imagined he would move to *STAR*, and then to Brussels, and from there to the denomination's headquarters in Springfield, Missouri, where he would touch a generation of missionaries and church leaders as he became Director of U.S. Relations for Assemblies of God World Missions.

A Place for People, Puppets, and Cockroach Soup

"TELL YOUR ENEMIES ABOUT THE LOVE OF JESUS."
"CUENTALE DEL AMOR DE CRISTO A TUS ENEMIGOS."

14

Carl

May I help with duplication and marketing?

1982

Carl and Geraldine Hultgren were practically at retirement age. For thirty years, they had been missionaries first in Brazil and then in Miami, Florida, at Life Publishers International. Four of their children were grown and away from home; only "the baby," David, a teenager, lived with them. Now, at age 61, Carl looked forward, not backward, and he saw children watching television and being changed by what they saw. He called Joe and asked if we needed help. Soon, the Hultgrens became "Uncle Carl and Aunt Gerry" to our cast and crew.

Carl and Gerry Hultgren

I am amazed at how God shifts people around—like a cosmic chess game. He moves this piece left, another piece forward. He shuffles, coordinates, and repositions thousands of us, all at the same time. Even as He dispatched David Lee to Europe, He scooted others toward us.

I Samuel 10:26 seemed to jump out at me: "… and the valiant men whose hearts God had touched went with him (Saul)." This reaffirmed to me that God would send us exactly the people we needed for this particular point in time. Even though I knew this would be true, going through times of transition is very hard for me.

I love to organize almost anything, so I loved being producer of *Lugar Secreto*. I typed the formats, assigned segments, scheduled the calendar, and coordinated the entire shoot. And as floor director, I reassured the talent, assisted the puppeteers, relayed the director's demands to the talent, and tried to keep both the control room and "the floor" happy.

Joe and I both felt totally fulfilled at STAR. He could use his skills of carpentry to design and build sets; he could minister in Spanish. He acquired puppeteering techniques with an innate ability to cause the puppets to "come alive." Joe traveled to raise funds; he called and conversed with pastors for hours to ask for offerings for special projects. He contacted our headquarters time after time for permission to expand our ministry or to purchase additional equipment and supplies.

The pressure on both of us was intense. Relentless. We focused, totally, on the task at hand. Anything else seemed trivial, insipid, without eternal purpose. STAR became both wife and mistress: gratifying and demanding. For ten years nothing else existed, only ministry through STAR.

***

"Norm, quit wiggling while I'm putting make-up on your white legs!" I giggled.

"Well, I didn't know being dressed-up like a Roman soldier meant I would have to get make-up smeared on my legs!" growled Norman Lestarjette.

Norm's wife, Marty, helped me sponge bronze make-up on Norm. We were out-of-doors, on location, to shoot an Easter program with Juan Romero, who had returned to host this special show.

I could hear his daughters singing in Spanish, rehearsing a trio with Crysti. Their voices blended beautifully.

This "Easter Special" would be edited and duplicated and sent to the twelve countries then airing *Lugar Secreto*. We were sure they would air it for free, too, just as they did the children's program and *Nueva Vida* (*New Life*).

***

Juan Romero singing on *Lugar Secreto*,
puppeteers hidden under the hillside

We took advantage of having Juan "back" as it gave us an opportunity to record lots of songs for *Lugar Secreto*.

He perched on the puppets' hillside and sang until he was hoarse. I think we placed around him every puppet that Fredda had sent to us.

Sue's flats looked really good in the background, adding color and depth to the hillside scene.

Toni with Juan

***

Several weeks later, Joe shouted over his shoulder as he flew out the front door, "Carl's here to pick me up. Meet you at Ernest Holbrook's church."

Joe and Carl drove to the U-Haul rental lot to pick up the largest truck available. From there, they would begin a circular round-up of sets and flats and props and puppets. First to Longfellow Boulevard to the old, empty house the Peninsular Florida District let us use for set storage.

At the old house, Carl and Joe loaded our tall flats and large sets into the truck. Then they drove to an air-conditioned storage unit to pick up the puppets and from there to another extra-space-in-someone's-storage unit to gather props. Finally, they stopped back by our house to pick up items from the garage.

We arrived at today's "shoot-site-borrowed-church" and began to unload. The guys arranged the larger set pieces while Aunt Gerry and I carried boxes and puppets, decorations and paperwork. Shooting in churches gave us lots of area to spread props on pews, but it also meant that, once again, we would have to clean up everything for the Wednesday night service, and pack everything back into the rental truck for the week-end.

When we finished shooting these shows, we would "tear down," dismantle the sets, clean up the borrowed facility, and return all our stuff to the storage units.

The Channel 22 building was nearly completed and Studio C was designated for our use. But before we even moved in, we were outgrowing it. Clearly, we needed a carpenter shop, space for prop storage, and offices all at the same location.

So, after 3-1/2 years, Joe began to search for a permanent home for *Star Productions*. He toured every decrepit old "warehouse" he could find. We needed a high ceiling. We needed air-conditioned office space. We needed a large storage space for props and sets. We needed it to be *inexpensive*!

Finally, in January, 1982, Joe called Hubert Wallace, who lived near Tampa in Durant, Florida, a tiny hamlet with a small post office, two little convenience stores, and a blinking yellow light at the only crossroads. Wallace served as pastor of Pleasant Grove Assembly of God, Joe's home church. Joe knew the church owned forty acres of beautiful country land. The area was quiet and peaceful, landscaped with palm trees and dozens of old oak trees draped in gray Spanish moss.

Joe explained our need, and immediately Pastor Wallace said, "Joe, you are welcome to come here. Put up a building. We'll even give you $6000 to help you pour the foundation. We'll draw up a contract indicating 'no charge.'"

We had noticed in Lakeland at the "Main Street" church, out behind the dumpster, a 30'x50' metal building in pieces leaning against a tree. Joe asked Pastor Strader about it. Could we have it? We would assemble it on our new property (yeah!) for our office space. The church donated it to us.

We shopped for prices for a 50'x50'x20' metal building for a studio. We could join the two buildings.

Six months later, the electricity was turned on in our shell of a building—two days before the large Channel 22 truck pulled up to shoot our next series of *Lugar Secreto*.

Construction begins

***

Carl strutted around like a proud turkey with his feathers extended. These "latter years" would be some of his best ministry ever! He loved to give tours. He would take visitors to see the props and puppets and electronic equipment. When he arrived at a spot where we especially needed something, Carl would pause, mention the exact amount the equipment would cost, and then turn to the visitor and say, "Would you pray that God will touch someone's heart to provide this equipment?" The visitor would pray and then, before leaving, would usually hand Carl a check.

Carl said, "Joe, we need to change our name from *STAR Productions* to *STAR Ministries*." And we did.

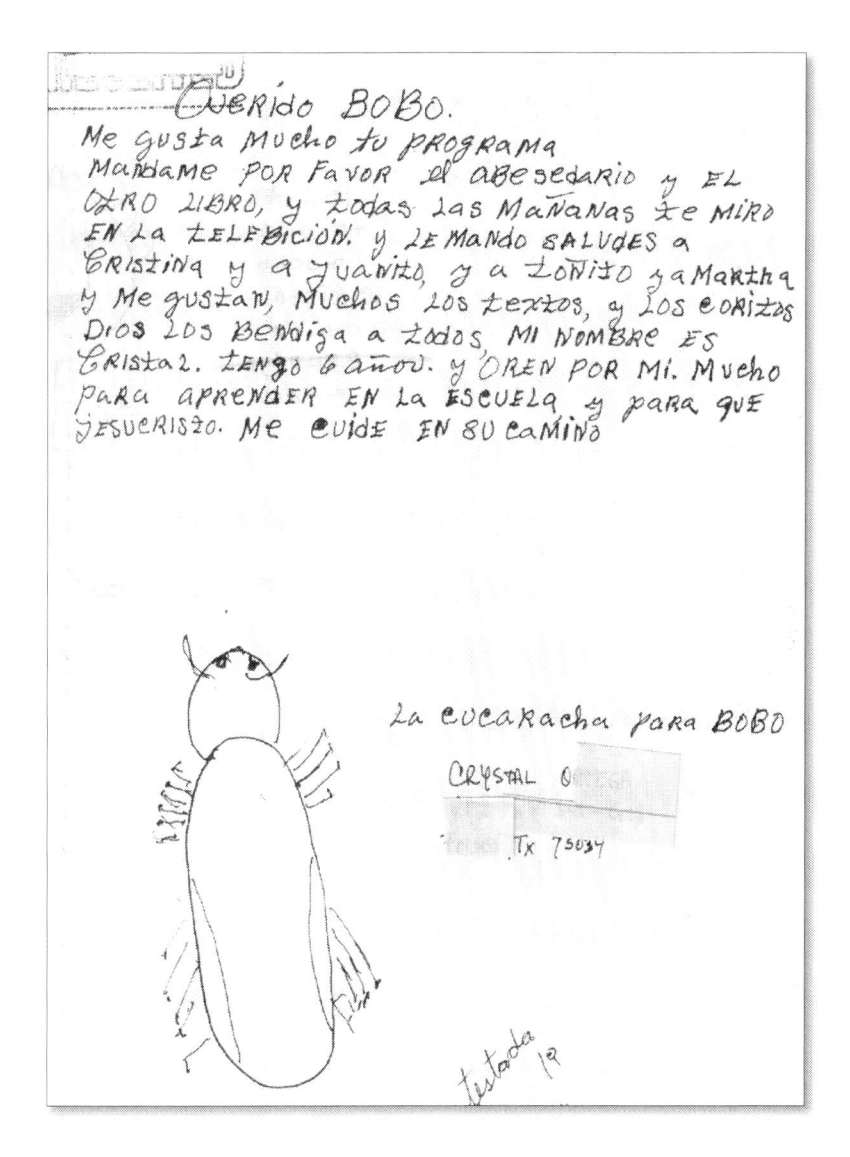

> Querido BOBO.
> Me gusta mucho tu programa mandame por favor el abesedario y el otro libro, y todas las mañanas te miro en la telebicion. y le mando saludes a Cristina y a Juanito, y a Toñito y a Martha y me gustan, muchos los textos, y los coritos Dios los bendiga a todos. Mi nombre es Cristal. Tengo 6 años. y oren por mi. mucho para aprender en la escuela y para que Jesucristo. Me cuide en su camino
>
> La cucaracha para BOBO
> CRYSTAL O
> Tx 75034

"Dear Bobo, I really like your program. Please send me the book. Every morning I watch you on television. Please greet Cristina, Juanito, Toñito, and Martha. I really like the Bible verses and the songs. God bless you all. My name is Cristal, I am 6 years old. Pray for me a lot so I can understand stuff at school, and so that Jesus Christ will keep me in his care. Here's a *cucaracha* (cockroach) for Bobo. Crystal."

JESUS LOVES LEWIS AND JENNY.
CRISTO AMA A LUIS Y A GINET.

15

Bruce

I volunteer to run camera.

1982-1983

How do you take a rag-tag bunch of part-time volunteers, with totally different backgrounds and skills, and mold them into a television production team? I don't know. But somehow we did. Year after year.

Bruce Page, an amateur photographer in his early twenties, took to the video camera like a duck to water.

Bruce panned and zoomed and trucked and tilted like a pro. He applied for MAPS appointment, (short-term missionary appointment), and came to STAR full-time.

Carl designated Bruce the "tech" to duplicate tapes when we weren't shooting programs. But we didn't actually have a real duplication area, yet, in our new building. In fact, everything and everybody operated out of the 30'x50' "office metal building." It was a shell, with a concrete floor. No drywall. No studs up yet. We decided that installing rest rooms was the first priority. Volunteers came, and they studded, drywalled, tiled, and plumbed.

Joe sat in a folding chair at a card table. I used our 90-days-same-as-cash-desk. Somehow we heard about some "free executive desks." We ended up with four huge, beat-up, extremely heavy, gray metal desks. It took four men to move one, inch by inch.

We butted all but one of our desks together in the middle of the room and made our own cubicles by attaching corkboards at the edge of our desks, between us. We had only one phone attached to a very long cord.

Within a few months, Roland and Evelyn Blount joined us (more about that in the next chapter). Whenever Joe would call our Missions Board to ask permission for one thing or another, everyone could hear—very clearly—the conversation and would pass notes to Joe to "ask about this, too." We placed the extra desk against the back side of our new drywall for the rest rooms, and Bruce used it for the duplication work.

Bruce Page

Then we brought the two 3/4" VCRs from our garage-room, and Bruce ran the machines all day every day, making copies to fulfill the standing orders. We also received numerous requests for Beta and VHS tapes for neighborhood Bible Clubs and home groups.

Because our "open" offices shared the one large, shell-of-a-room, and because Bruce was running the video tape recorders day after day, we could all hear the Spanish programs over and over and over again. One day, exasperated, Carl got up from his desk, walked briskly over to Bruce and pleaded, "Boy, would you *please* turn that down?" The next day, Carl did the same thing and the day after that, and the day after that, too. We would start to smile as soon as we heard Carl's footsteps heading in Bruce's direction, and we would all mouth the words, "Boy, would you *please* turn that down?"

***

We began to receive heartwarming feedback on our productions. In February, 1982, *Lugar Secreto* received from Hollywood, California, the highest award in Christian television: an *Angel Award*. Two other producers from Channel 22 did also: Arthelene Rippy for her singles' show, *Solo Act*; and Don MacAllister for his English children's show, *Joy Junction*. For the following ten years, we submitted shows, and every year we were awarded the beautiful little *Silver Angel* statue, the highest media award in our category.

Joe, Arthelene Rippy, and Don MacAllister
with one of the Silver Angel Awards

A letter came from John Wilkie in Guayaquil, Ecuador: "We have received over 200 letters to *Lugar Secreto*. We have started eight prayer cells as a result of these contacts, plus write-ins to the *Nueva Vida* series and the *Spanish PTL Club* with Juan Romero."

The director of an orphanage in Colonia V. Guerrero, Mexico, wrote a letter that brought tears to our eyes. The children dearly loved *Lugar Secreto* and watched it every day. Could *Cristina* please come for a visit? Enclosed with the director's letter were seventy letters from the children, each letter sporting colorful drawings of Bobo, his *cucarachas,* Tomasito, Rosita, Judy, and Cristina.

Crysti flew to the Baja Peninsula, where area missionaries met her. They headed south, driving for over an hour in arid countryside. They bumped over cobblestones, through the gates, down the orphanage driveway. Dozens of kids, eyes aglow, watched *Cristina* climb out of the car. One by one, as they hugged her, they expressed their love in rapid-fire Spanish. Cristina hugged each child tightly, hardly believing the joy of touching these little lives in ways she could never have imagined. She assured the kids that just as soon as she returned to the *Lugar Secreto,* she would say hello for them to Bobo and Judy and Rosita and Tomasito.

***

Bruce Page is a great example of many volunteers who blessed us in so many ways. When Bruce stood behind the camera, he looked through the lens and saw people hungry for the Good News. As he ran the duplicating machines, Bruce wanted to do more than just send tapes. When he held up a puppet, his heart stirred for foreign missions. He wanted to *go*. And eventually he did! As I write these words, Bruce, with his wife, Joy, and their children, serve as missionaries in Northern Europe.

Bruce and Tim on camera, Sue's flats in background

16

Roland

I can't see those little red lights!

1983, Paraguay

"No way, José," Roland emphasized to Joe. "There is no way I'm leaving Paraguay ... I've been here for ten years ... I won't even consider transferring to STAR."

On Valentine's Day, 1983, Joe and I sat in Paraguay around the dining table with Roland and Evelyn Blount. They had invited us down to spend a week filming the tremendous outpouring of God's Spirit in that little country.

During our four years in Paraguay, its churches were few, with only a small number of believers. Now yellow and white tents dotted the barrios where, every evening, hundreds of people gathered to hear the gospel. Under the leadership of Loren Triplett, C.W. VanDolsen directed a host of missionaries and lay preachers. Jan and Victor Hedman, missionaries who had transferred up from Argentina, flourished in ministry in Paraguay, even helping to establish a new church of thousands of believers. Jan told me, "Most of the people I interview first heard the Gospel on *Las Buenas Nuevas* television program that you and Roland began here. Your program broke down centuries-old prejudices—it has changed a generation."

Roland served as pastor of a wonderful congregation in the church we had started together in 1976 at the Bible school campus. But, he had resigned as pastor the previous Sunday and had already turned the church over to a young man he had mentored.

"Roland, you can clearly see the value of television," Joe continued, pressing his point. "We need you at STAR. I need you to run audio in our new studio. We touched thousands of Paraguayans with the television program we produced together here. You continued, after I left, augmenting the impact. Now you have an opportunity to touch tens of thousands of Latinos all over Latin America. We touched a country. Now we can touch a continent."

"Thanks. But no thanks," Roland repeated as we pushed our chairs under the dining room table and headed upstairs to take a traditional Paraguayan siesta.

As soon as their bedroom door closed, Evelyn turned to Roland. "You know," she paused, "we have not even prayed about whether or not to accept Joe's invitation."

"I don't need to pray. I don't *want* to pray. I want to stay here in Paraguay," Roland reaffirmed.

Soon, Evelyn drifted off to sleep. Roland, who always enjoyed his siesta, tossed and turned. Finally, he began to pray, "God, I know You don't want us to move. Surely You don't ... do You?"

And without hearing a voice or seeing a vision, Roland *knew*. He just *knew*. The knowledge filled his chest and dampened his cheeks with tears.

That evening Roland asked, "Joe, how soon do you need me?"

"Within a couple of months. We're ready to put up the drywall for the control room. We need you to run audio for the *Lugar Secreto* shoot in July."

"Loren (our Foreign Missions Director) is actually in Paraguay for a few days," Roland said. "I'll ask for permission to transfer." A tiny flicker of excitement began to flutter under Roland's ribs.

But he continued with one more question, "What does the Peninsular Florida District think of having 'foreign missionaries' stationed there in Florida?"

"They seem to love it! I have letters from the Superintendent, J. Foy Johnson, and the Treasurer, Ray Schultz, welcoming us and opening the District to us. The pastors could not be more affirming—I have visited almost every church. The pastors allow me to present our ministry and our needs, then the churches respond with generous offerings. Many churches provide housing in a nice hotel, and church members even volunteer to help at STAR."

Two months later, Roland walked into the STAR building. Evelyn had remained in Paraguay for a few more weeks until their daughter, Carla, could finish the school year. Roland entered the building with confidence. Our boss, Loren, had asked only one question, "Can you run the audio board?" To which Roland had replied, "Sure, I run the sound system here all the time."

Joe led Roland into the new control room. "Here's the Peavey. It's simple to run, you just learn one channel; all the channels are the same." Joe took Roland's hand and ran it over the audio board. The board went on and on and on. Channel after channel after channel.

Roland gasped, "How many channels does this board have?"

"Twenty-four."

"Twenty-four!? I didn't dream such a thing existed! My audio board had six channels! How many buttons are on this thing!?"

They counted over 300 buttons, knobs, and slides.

"Roland, hey, don't panic. To know the audio levels, you just watch these little red lights."

All at once, both men realized that Roland could not run the board. He could not see the little red lights. Roland is totally blind.

Both men felt a wave of despair. Joe had invited Roland to transfer to STAR. Roland had thought God was leading him to leave his beloved Paraguay, to come here—to be an utter failure.

Just at that moment, a disheveled kid—an intern from Southeastern College—walked into the control room. His sandy brown, tousled hair fell in his eyes; large safety pins held up his raveling jeans while the pant legs dragged along the floor. "What's the problem here?" Scott asked. He wanted to be a video engineer and already knew a lot about electronics. With a heavy heart, Joe and Roland explained the problem. "I'll be back in a little while," Scott murmured, and disappeared.

Two hours later, Scott handed Roland a little black, plastic box about the size of a slice of bread folded in half. A small rubber tube protruded from one side; a toggle switch stuck out the other side.

"All right, let's try this. Turn the battery on with the toggle. Put the little hose over the diode, the red light. When it lights up, the box will beep and you'll know the level is correct."

Scott had gone to Radio Shack and for less than $10.00 had bought the little empty plastic box, a light sensor, a beeper, a battery, a little rubber hose, and a toggle switch. Scott had invented a gadget that would revolutionize Roland's life and would change televiewers' lives around the world.

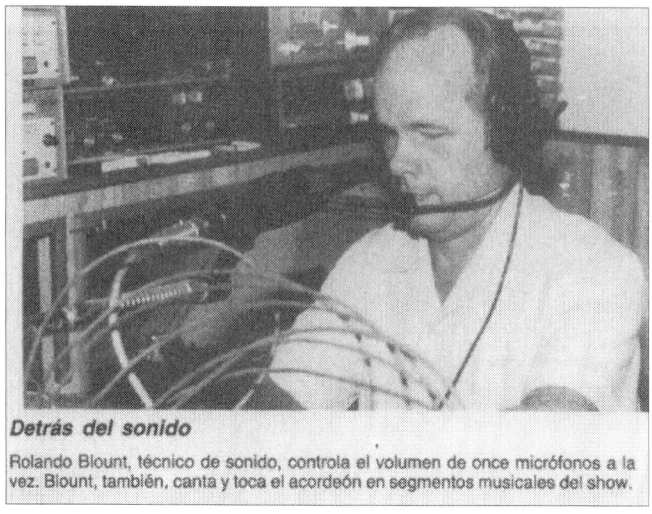

Detrás del sonido

Rolando Blount, técnico de sonido, controla el volumen de once micrófonos a la vez. Blount, también, canta y toca el acordeón en segmentos musicales del show.

A Spanish newspaper featured Roland at the soundboard

    July would be our first production without the help of Channel 22. Paul Garber had received missionary appointment and had moved to Belgium to be video engineer for a sister ministry there.

    We maintained a wonderful relationship with Channel 22, but we were ready to try our wings. So, although we were scared of shooting alone, we were confident, too. We had learned so much. Speed-the-Light had bought cameras and all the supporting electronics for us. Scott had wired our new control room. We were all set to shoot this series!

    Roland's hands were sweaty as he toggled the switch on the black box and placed it over the little red light. Time for mike checks. "Testing, 1, 2." Roland adjusted the levels. Not only did Roland have six puppeteer mikes to control all at the same time, he also needed to cue the theme music for each segment on the cart machine, or the turntable, and the reel to reel. "Stand by. Roll tape. Tape is rolling. 10, 9, 8, 7 ...."

    By the end of July, we finished shooting almost 100 segments. Not one time did we have to stop and repeat because of a slip-up on

Roland's part. We had stopped; we had started over, several times, but not because of an audio problem.

When the month ended, Roland confessed, "I was really nervous heading into this production month. But one day when I was reading my Spanish Bible, Isaiah 49:23 stood out to me. I read it several times. There are shades of meaning between the English and the Spanish. In Spanish it says, 'They that wait or hope in the Lord will never be embarrassed.'" Roland's voice cracked, "That was *my verse*. You never had to stop because of me. I was not embarrassed. Not even once."

United in heart with Carl, Bruce, Roland and Evelyn, we talked often of our philosophy. We were a ministry. We were not a business. We were *not* in the business of selling tapes. If we could recoup our cost-per-tape, fine, but we would make the programs available to the missionaries free of charge, or nearly free. We would bear the burden of raising money for production costs and building expenses. This was part of our ministry to the other missionaries.

***

By the end of 1983, we had produced 132 programs and sent 1,746 copies to 50 missionaries. Our potential audience reached 50 million people spanning 22 countries. All with a handful of missionaries and a rag-tag group of part-time volunteers enabled by the Holy Spirit of God.

After previewing one of our shows, a professional video producer told Philip Hogan, Executive Director of Foreign Missions, "Those people cannot be producing this quality of programming with so few people and so little equipment."

"READ AND HIDE GOD'S WORD IN YOUR HEART!"
"¡LEE Y GUARDA EN TU CORAZON LA PALABRA DE DIOS!"

17

Evelyn

Move that plant two inches to the left.

"We need some black cloth to cover that puppeteer's head. And move that big silk plant two inches to the left," Evelyn called loudly from behind her camera. She wanted every shot from *her* camera to be perfect.

Evelyn had decided when she and Roland moved to STAR that she would probably stay at home. Mostly. Well, she *could* help with bookkeeping. Part-time. Then, one day during lunch break, Evelyn went into the studio and began to practice running camera. She loved it! She became excellent on camera and especially loved to operate the boom-camera where she could shoot from any angle.

We continued with the children's shows, but we also wanted discipleship programs for adults. We worked with *The Christian Training Network* in Latin America, and with *International Correspondence Institute*. Both entities had excellent printed material, and we helped them to put quality teaching on video. So, within a few months, Evelyn added "producer" to her skills. She produced dozens of these educational courses for pastors, the laity, and college students. Some courses were Bible studies, and some were practical helps for men and women who wanted to be pastors but could not afford to leave home to attend a Bible college.

Because Roland is blind, he and Evelyn felt keenly the need for good quality *audio*. One of his favorite sayings is, "In television, we produce good audio, and just enhance it with video." Back in Paraguay, he had produced radio programs for two years from his home.

Every morning at 5:30, he was "live" via telephone lines to one of the most powerful radio stations in the nation. Even the bus drivers played his devotionals as the commuters headed to work on the overcrowded buses.

So, from his first days at STAR, Roland looked for radio opportunities. Therefore, during a well-known evangelist's heyday, Roland spent hundreds of hours extracting from the evangelist's hour-long television shows the Spanish audio by translator Stanley Black. Roland edited the clips into 30-minute radio programs. Roland was so proficient that a person could not distinguish his edit points. By the end of 1985, we had distributed 6,789 radio programs.

But not just stuff for adults—Roland and Evelyn wanted *kids' radio shows*, too. Sarita wrote the scripts, Evelyn produced the shows, and Roland recorded them: *Los Vecinitos de Arbolandia* (*The Neighbors in Treelandia*), where the characters from *Lugar Secreto* came alive on audio. They would eventually record ninety-six 15-minute shows.

Cast and Crew of *Los Vecinitos* in Colombia

Between video shoots of *Lugar Secreto*, Roland and Evelyn and Crysti would travel to Colombia, South America, to tape *Los Vecinitos* with Maritza, Sarita, Judy, and some new puppeteers, Carlos and Amanda Luna and William Bustos. (I'll tell about them in another chapter).

Evelyn gave of herself totally to ministry. And to assist Roland. Her life has not been an easy one, always having to transport Roland, always needing to be "his eyes." But never once in the decades that I have known her, never *once* have I heard her complain about it. When Roland needs to go somewhere, he says, "Let me check with my chauffeur; I'll get back to you."

***

Missionary Janie Boulware-Wead, just back from Spain, joined us for a year to produce in Spanish a series of practical teaching for new pastors.

One day, coming out of the studio building, Janie screamed so loudly that we all went running to see what had happened. Janie stood, paralyzed, while a long, blacksnake drooped in front of her face, slid off the top of the door frame, and gently wrapped itself across her shoulders.

But snakes did not deter Janie. She worked with her mentor, Evelyn, to learn television production. The same Evelyn who almost just stayed at home.

Janie as Floor Director, Joe, and an intern from Angola
(Please excuse Bobo; he passed out on the table.)

A Place for People, Puppets, and Cockroach Soup

"I HAVE AN APPLE AND *SOME* FRUIT TO SHARE."
"TENGO UNA MANZANA Y OTRAS FRUTAS QUE PUEDO COMPARTIR."

18

Hilda

Who wants some carrot salad?

"How much longer to the end of this segment?" whispered Hilda, standing in the shadows watching the "shoot." "About ten minutes," I whispered back, covering the mouthpiece of my floor-director's headset. "All right. Dinner will be served in fifteen minutes: country fried steak, mashed potatoes, gravy, corn, black-eyed peas, strawberry shortcake, and Joe's favorite carrot salad," Hilda replied with a twinkle in her eye, her dimple shining. She knew Joe hated carrot salad. She continued, "I'll be waiting in the church cafeteria."

Evelyn is the one who suggested we call Hilda, her cousin. "She's a great cook. Why don't we see if she would help us just this one time?" Poor Hilda did not know what had hit her! She was in for years of hard labor.

I have heard that "an army runs on its stomach," meaning that troops can fight only as long as they have strength. Well, our physical strength came by way of Hilda Swindal.

Her domain was the church cafeteria, which sat adjacent to our STAR building. The Pleasant Grove church began as a brush-arbor camp meeting. People built cabins surrounding the "tabernacle" and then closed-in the "church" and remodeled the cabins to become year-round residences.

We were really grateful to be able to use the cafeteria year 'round—except during the old fashioned camp meeting each fall. But even then, we could join the campers and eat the good southern cooking the church cooks, including Hilda, prepared.

Hilda at work in the cafeteria

Hilda and all of our cast and crew learned quickly that in television production, you hurry up and wait. You hurry into position, and then you wait for a light to be adjusted, or for mike checks, or for a puppeteer to get an extra pillow for his elbow. In fact, we had learned, very quickly, that ninety percent of our television ministry was not actually "shooting" at all. To produce TV programs, you have to make all the plans, build the sets, accumulate props—this is called *pre-production*.

Then you actually shoot the shows. This is called *production*.

After that, you edit, copy, and distribute the programs. This is called *post-production*.

To our great surprise, *production* occupied only about ten percent of our total time. The other ninety percent we spent in *pre-production, post-production*, and in raising funds.

Many times at STAR, we doubled as both cast and crew. (As I mentioned in "TV Terms" at the beginning of this book, the word "cast" refers to people who are actually seen on the show; "crew" are the behind-the-scenes people who make it happen: they run cameras and audio, set lights, and assemble the sets.) Because many of our cast and crew were college students or worked in school settings, we set summertime and Christmas holidays as our major *production* times for *Lugar Secreto*. This meant that for one month, twice a year, the STAR studio bulged with people. We worked hard from early mornings until late evenings. How could we sustain our energy? How could we prepare food (and snacks) for all of us while we were "out on the studio floor" shooting?

Incredibly, that is when Hilda came to our rescue. She fed twenty to thirty of us on a shoe-string budget. She commandeered volunteer cooks; she persuaded church members to empty their freezers of frozen foods and donate vegetables fresh from their gardens. Hilda could bake chicken tetrazzini that would melt in your mouth, or mac and cheese, or umm...that delicious baked chicken with the crispy coating. Lunch was called dinner, and dinner was called supper-leftovers.

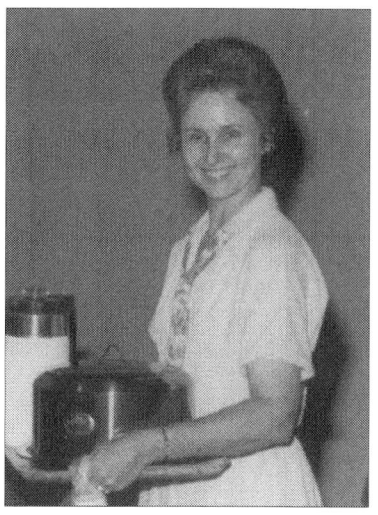

Do you see the twinkle in Hilda's eye?

Hilda took over the church cafeteria and served us as we walked down the line beside the steam table. She had a quick smile and a twinkle in her eye for every dip of potatoes for every person. Day after day. Month after month. Year after year. Hilda worked long, hot hours, cooking and cleaning up the cafeteria not only for the large *Lugar Secreto* shoots, but also for the educational productions. She and her volunteers received no pay. I have never known anyone with more of a servant spirit than Hilda.

She's in heaven now, probably in charge of cooking for some big event the Lord is planning.

Hilda's Chicken Tetrazzini

Printed in the Pleasant Grove Cook Book, 1992 edition, Durant, FL

Bake about 20 minutes at 375 degrees

INGREDIENTS

    1 chicken, cooked and boned
    2 cans cream of mushroom soup
    1 can mushrooms (8 oz)
    1 package angel-hair pasta (1 lb)
    1 medium jar chopped pimientos
    1 large package shredded cheese (or cheese slices)
    Chicken broth
    Salt and pepper to taste

PREPARATION

Cook chicken, cool, and remove from bone. Save broth.

Cook pasta *just* until barely tender. Drain.

Mix soup, mushrooms, chicken and pasta, salt, pepper, and pimientos. Add enough broth so it won't cook dry.

Place in a 9x13 casserole dish with cheese on top. Bake at 375 degrees until cheese melts, about 20 minutes.

Ice cream, anyone?
Olan and Charles help the ice cream man.

"BOBO, PEOPLE NEVER EAT COCKROACHES!"
"¡BOBO, LA GENTE NUNCA COME CUCARACHAS!"

19

Bobo's Favorite Recipes

Try my delicious soup!

Cristina always walks into the show, *El Lugar Secreto* (*Secret Place*), to find Bobo hard at work on some project. He may be cooking up a scientific experiment with smoke curling and circuits flickering on and off. Or he may be wearing his chef's hat and be holding his big wooden spoon while he stirs some concoction in his battered cooking pot. On one show, he waved his spoon under Cristina's nose, "Here, try my soup."

"No, thank you. Knowing you, I'm sure you put *great big* roaches in that soup."

"No, I didn't," Bobo declared vehemently. "Here, try a bite." Bobo held out the big wooden spoon.

Cristina took a bite. "Auuuhhh. Horrible! Bobo! You said there were no roaches in that soup!"

"I said there were no *big* roaches in this soup—there are lots of *little* roaches. Ha, ha, ha, ha."

One time, Bobo stole cockroaches from his neighbor's house to put in his soup ... he (and the children watching) learned that a person should not steal. Another time, he lied about what was in the soup, and he learned a lesson in honesty.

Sometimes when Bobo asks the children to write in to receive a free coloring book, he says, "It's free. Just send me a roach or two." Well, in numerous countries, the children included roaches in their letters! The secretaries screamed the first time they opened a letter ... and then, after that, *very carefully*, opened Bobo's mail.

If you would rather not try Bobo's favorite soup (6 to 8 plastic cockroaches per cup of water), here are some other recipes, his family's favorites.

Aunt Paula's Broccoli Casserole
Bake about 20 minutes at 375 degrees

INGREDIENTS
> Fresh or frozen broccoli (see Preparation)
> 1/2 block of the large Velveeta cheese (or one small package)
> 1/3 can low-fat evaporated milk
> 1/2 cup skimmed milk
> 3 tablespoons flour
> Several shakes Tabasco sauce
> 1 teaspoon mustard (powder or sandwich style)
> 1 can French Fried Onion Rings

PREPARATION

Two large bags of frozen broccoli: one of broccoli buds and one of regular frozen broccoli. (If you use all buds, it is not as good, but the regular frozen broccoli has too many stems.)

Microwave about two or three cups of frozen broccoli at a time until fork tender (covered, with a tablespoon of water).

Place cooked broccoli in a 9x13 casserole dish. Keep microwaving more broccoli until the casserole dish is full.

In your microwave dish, chip 1/2 block of low-fat Velveeta. Add 1/3 can low-fat evaporated milk, several shakes of Tabasco sauce, 3 tablespoons of flour, 1/2 cup skimmed milk, and the mustard.

Microwave the cheese mixture, stopping every few minutes to whip with a whisk. Continue until it becomes a smooth cheese sauce. (Don't make it too thick or it won't cover broccoli well—add milk if needed.)

Pour the cheese sauce over the broccoli. Spread onion rings on top. Bake at 375 degrees until it browns and is bubbly around the edges. (about 20 minutes)

Crysti's Tex-Mex Chili

INGREDIENTS
    4 lbs ground beef (ask butcher to grind stew beef for you)
    1 large yellow onion, chopped
    1 large sweet (white) onion, chopped
    1 green pepper, chopped
    1 head fresh garlic, crushed (not just a clove!)
    2 cans refried beans
    1 can black beans
    4 cans original Rotel tomatoes (it is very spicy)
    2 cans (4 cups if fresh) chopped tomatoes
    1 small can tomato paste
    2 bottles Corona beer
    2 small cans sliced (or small whole) black olives
    2 tablespoons lime juice
    1 tablespoon Chipotle hot sauce
    1 tube frozen creamed corn (optional)
    Cayenne pepper, to your taste
    1 tablespoon cumin
    1/2 cup chopped cilantro
    1 tablespoon brown sugar
    Salt and pepper, to taste

TOPPINGS: Shredded cheddar cheese, shredded Monterey Jack cheese, sour cream, chopped green onions, chopped cilantro

SERVE WITH: Corn tortilla chips, Fritos, or softened corn tortillas

PREPARATION: Brown meat. Add chopped vegetables. Sauté. Add remaining ingredients. Bring to a boil. Simmer, uncovered, 'til you can't stand it any longer!

    Give each person a bowl of "soup" and an individual bowl or basket of chips and tortillas to use as "scoops." No spoons allowed!

Aunt Jan's Chicken Enchilada Casserole
Bake at 350 degrees for 50 minutes

INGREDIENTS
- 11 corn tortillas, cut into quarters
- 5 cups cooked chicken, diced
- 3 cups shredded cheese, cheddar or Mexican mix
- 2 cans Rotel tomatoes (1 for the sauce, 1 to spread on top)

Sauce:
- 1 1/2 cups chicken broth
- 1 can condensed cream of mushroom soup
- 1 can condensed cream of chicken soup (or cream of celery)
- 1 can Rotel tomatoes
- 1/2 cup sliced black olives (small can)
- 4 oz. chopped green chilies (small can)
- 1/3 cup chopped onions (or 4 green onions, chopped)

PREPARATION
1. Boil chicken in water with some garlic, maybe a stick of celery, half an onion. (Remove celery and onion later.) You can use chicken breasts, but use at least some pieces with skin-on, for a better flavor. It will take about 6 breasts or one small chicken plus 3 boneless breasts. Chop cooked chicken. Save broth. (If you have extra broth, it freezes well.)
2. Slice tortillas into quarters.
3. Sauce: Mix the condensed soups with little bits of the broth until it is all mixed well. Then add the remaining ingredients to the sauce.
4. Layer ingredients (as for lasagna) into 9x13 casserole dish/pan. Oil the pan, then spread a little sauce on the bottom of the pan. Place one layer of tortilla pieces on top of sauce. Try not to double tortillas on each other, or they might not get soft while cooking.
5. Sprinkle tortilla layer with 1/3 of the chicken. Cover with 1/3 of the sauce. Sprinkle with 1/3 of the cheese. Try to get some sauce or cheese on every bit of the tortillas so they will become moist.
6. Repeat two more layers: tortillas, chicken, sauce, cheese.
7. Top with grated cheese and the other can of Rotel tomatoes (juice and all).

Bake until good and bubbly. About 50 minutes at 350 degrees.

Grandma Duckie's Spanish Bean Soup

Aunt Irma and Aunt Bootie made their own special variations
(makes 8 to 10 generous servings)

INGREDIENTS

- 2 cans garbanzo beans
- 2 links Kiel-basa sausage (Polish or Spanish—I use one "hot" link)
- 1 green pepper, chopped
- 1 large onion, chopped
- 6 buds garlic, chopped fine
- 6 medium potatoes, chopped into cubes
- 6 small cans chicken broth (or equivalent)
- Tabasco sauce
- 1 cardboard (4 packets) Vigo seasoning for yellow rice
- 1 bay leaf
- 1 tablespoon Italian seasoning
- Salt
- A very large cooking pot

PREPARATION

I love to prepare this because everything goes into the pot at the same time! It simmers for several hours and fills the house with a delicious aroma.

1. Split the kielbasa sausage lengthwise. Then split it again. (To get "fourths.") Slice into small pieces.
2. Peel and cube the potatoes.
3. Cube the onions and green pepper, and mince the garlic.
4. Place all the ingredients into a very large pot.
5. Add all 4 packets of the Vigo seasoning, and 3 or 4 dashes of Tabasco sauce. Add the bay leaf and Italian seasoning.
6. Cover with the broth. If there is not plenty of liquid, you might need to add a cup or two of water. If so, add a tablespoon of chicken bouillon.
7. Bring to a boil (it will take about half an hour because the pot will be so full). Simmer gently at least one hour. The longer it sits, the better it is.
8. Taste, and add a little salt, if needed. The broth is salty, so be careful.
9. NOTE: Great served with fresh Cuban bread or garlic bread.

Maggie's Famous Garlic Butter

INGREDIENTS
    2 beautiful, long, fresh loaves of French or Cuban bread
    Butter, margarine or Smart Balance is OK; one tub
    Garlic salt (not powder), about 1 tablespoon
    Paprika, about 1 tablespoon
    Parsley flakes, about 1 tablespoon

PREPARATION

Mix softened butter with the garlic salt, paprika, and parsley flakes until blended. Butter should be reddish from the paprika, with plenty of parsley flakes showing, and the butter should taste garlic-salty.

Split the bread lengthwise and cover to the very edges with the butter. Place pieces on a cookie sheet.

Heat the oven to about 400, and then, when you put the bread in, turn on the broiler. Broil until lightly browned. (If your oven isn't preheated, the bread won't get crispy on the bottom.) Or, if cooking a small amount, toast bread in a toaster oven.

Refrigerate any left-over garlic butter to use at a future time.

Maggie's "Southern" Iced Tea

I use 4 small tea bags to 1 cup sugar for an 8-cup pitcher.

Place tea bags in about 1 and 1/2 cups of boiling water. Cover and steep for 7 minutes.

Place 1 cup sugar into the pitcher. Pour the hot tea into the pitcher on top of the sugar. Stir well. Add more water to the tea bags, pour into pitcher. Continue until water runs clear. Then finish filling the pitcher with water. This procedure makes the sugar melt and gives the "southern" flavor.

Rhenda's Frappé

Bobo's cousin has made a drink "to die for" especially for those special occasions when you would serve punch.

INGREDIENTS
- 1 ounce instant coffee
- 1/2 cup sugar
- 1 quart very hot water
- 1 pint heavy whipping cream
- 3 half-gallons of soft vanilla ice cream
- cinnamon for garnish

PREPARATION
Dissolve coffee and sugar in hot water. Chill.
Pour coffee mixture into large bowl along with whipping cream.
Gently mix in ice cream. Some lumps may still remain when you have finished.
Sprinkle cinnamon on top of each serving, if desired.
Yields 25 small servings.

***

Inside Bobo's fridge

Tim's Ropa Vieja
Shredded Beef with Latino Flavor
(In his own words)

INGREDIENTS
- 2 flank steaks
- 3 green peppers, 1 yellow pepper, 1 red pepper (supermarkets often sell these peppers together)
- 3 to 4 onions
- 1 tablespoon cumin
- Gloop of olive oil
- 1 tablespoon chopped or minced garlic
- 3 cans diced tomatoes
- 1 can Rotel tomatoes
- 1 small can tomato paste
- 1 large jar pimientos or 2 of the small jars
- Small can green peas
- Tabasco
- Juice of one lime
- 1/2 cup cilantro, chopped
- Bay leaf or two
- 1/2 bottle Negra Modelo Dark beer. Drink the other half. (Be sure Mom is not watching!)

PREPARATION

Cut the 2 flank steaks into 1 inch strips WITH the grain, and then cut them into about 5-inch lengths.

Boil "the stuffin" out of them. At least an hour. I usually use beer for this, but I'm not convinced it makes much difference what you use to boil them in.

Meanwhile, cut the 3 green peppers, the yellow pepper and the red pepper into strips.

Cut the 3 to 4 onions into strips.

Put them all into your pot. I like to use our cast iron Dutch oven.

Add the remaining ingredients. Cook it all together on medium heat until meat starts to shred easily with a fork.

Shred the meat. I use tongs and a fork for this.

I think that's it! It's good with rice and Cuban bread, and also it makes delicious sandwiches.

Joe's Chocolate Turtles
(In his own words)

Joe's friend, Dave Norris, perfected this recipe.
His wife, Peggy, and Joe's wife, Maggie, stay out of the kitchen!

INGREDIENTS
- 1-1/2 tablespoons milk
- 8 oz. caramels
- 2 cups pecan halves
- 1-1/2 lbs. bark chocolate (Ghirardelli **bark**)
- Parchment paper (the turtles will stick to anything else)

PREPARATION

Step one: caramels and pecans
1. Melt caramels to stirrability in microwave **at half power**.
2. Mix in milk. Continue to melt until no lumps remain.
3. Stir in pecans, one cup at a time.
4. Drop 3 or 4 coated pecans onto parchment paper (on cookie sheets).
5. Cool. Place in freezer, if possible.

Step two: covering with chocolate
1. Melt chocolate **at half-power** or less.
2. Drop turtles (now cold) into chocolate, using tongs or two forks to immerse and remove.
3. Place turtles back onto the parchment paper.
4. Allow a few of them to harden before you start eating them!

NOTE: things Dave taught Joe
- "Pam" or oil all bowls and spoons.
- 36 caramels = 8 oz.
- 12 blocks chocolate = 1-1/2 lbs
- If chocolate won't liquefy, add a few drops of oil.
- Note the "bark" chocolate, nothing else works as well.

Tessa (Tim's daughter) making biscuits
G'eema Margaret is helping.

Granddaughters Kyndal, Tessa, Jennifer helping Papa Joe
(Kyndal and Jennifer, Crysti's daughters)

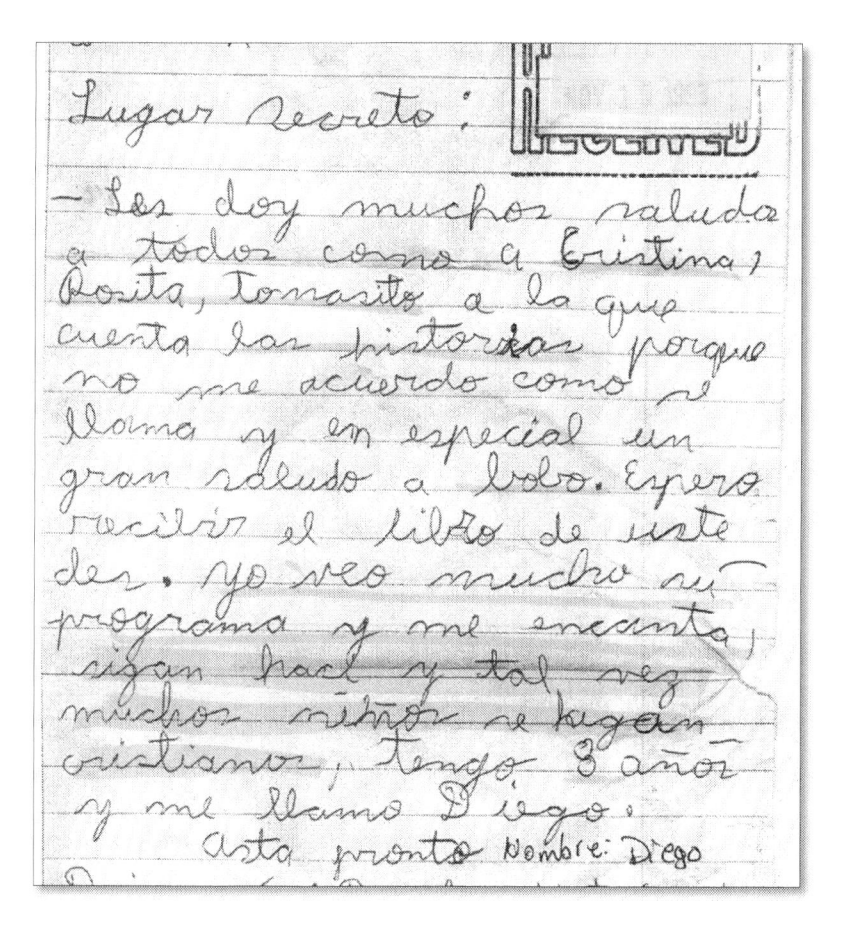

"*Lugar Secreto*: I give many greetings to everyone like Cristina, Rosita, Tomasito, and to the one who tells the stories .... And especially a big greeting to Bobo. I hope to receive the book from you. I watch your programs a lot and I love them. Keep on doing them and maybe many children will become Christians. I am 8 years old and my name is Diego. See you later, my name, Diego"

BOBO'S LETTER SAYS, "Jesus loves YOU!"
LA CARTA DE BOBO DICE: "¡Cristo te ama A TI!"

20

Red, Ed, and Fred-da

I sent you the tapes already.

1983—

Clutching a sheaf of mismatched papers, Winifred Dean sat hunched over her desk. "Red," as everyone called her, had reached retirement age and volunteered to be Carl's assistant to process the orders and ship the videos.

"C'mon, Red, time to quit for the day," I called, picking up my purse and heading toward the door.

"No, I can't leave. I am staying here with Artie Johnson until I figure out what on earth she means in this latest letter."

We laughed together, knowing full well that Red would be reading and re-reading for several hours.

Artie, a missionary in Durango, Mexico, had ordered all of our *Lugar Secreto* shows, plus all of the educational videos for the Bible institute there. But—tapes could only be sent one by one, so that Artie would not have to pay customs fees. Plus, many times the *Lugar Secreto* package of videos "disappeared" in transit.

So, typically, Artie would write, "Red, please re-send the last episode you sent two weeks ago. I did receive the other tape, though, the one you mailed the time before that. And, oh, yes, you don't need to send the educational teaching on the Holy Spirit, Lesson 6 ... I think, or did I already get that one? Anyway, the one that I mentioned last month, don't re-send because it just arrived." Poor Red sat for hours with Artie's enigmatic requests.

Winifred (Red) Dean

***

A few days later, Carl said that a friend, David M. Hansen, wanted a special meeting with us.

"Please produce your *Lugar Secreto* in English," he pleaded. "My grandkids need it, so do our neighbor kids, and the children who live down the street—and all children across the English-speaking world."

"Dave, we're foreign missionaries," replied Joe. "We cannot take time away from Spanish distribution to promote English shows, even if we received permission to produce them."

"I'll do it," Dave exclaimed. "I'll do all the distribution in English for you."

The idea stuck in our hearts. What if we used the same sets and shot an English version immediately after the Spanish segment? We decided to try one show, a pilot.

On July 13, 1983, Cristina came through the door into the *Secret Place*. She greeted the viewer in English. Then she said, "Hi, Bobo," and gave him a hug.

"Hola, Cristina," Bobo replied in *Spanish*. Take 2. Take 3. Finally, we decided Bobo would just have to be bilingual! He had been "born" speaking Spanish and it was very hard for Bobo (for Joe as Bobo) to "think" in English.

The pilot show was not too bad, and subsequently our mission gave us permission to produce in English—besides, we reasoned, the Caribbean countries needed English shows.

The cast on the *Secret Place* closing set
Shelby and Connie Lanier, Crysti, Bobo, Joe, Jenny Penhallegon

And, true to his word, David Hansen distributed thousands of *Secret Place* videos throughout the U.S. and Canada. He never would have dreamed that thirty years later those English videos would touch a new generation of children all over the world via satellites and be dubbed into Tamil and Hindi for broadcast in India.

***

At 2:00 p.m. on Friday, December 2, 1983, we dedicated the *STAR Ministries* building. Dignitaries J. Philip Hogan (World Missions Director), Loren Triplett (Latin American Missions Director), J. Foy Johnson (Superintendent, Peninsular Florida District), Gordon Matheny (District Official and Pastor), and veteran missionaries George Davis and Mamie Williams gave prayers, speeches, and cut the ribbon. Hundreds of people attended the open house on Saturday, December 3.

Dedication Day, December 2, 1983
Left to right: Carl Hultgren, Roland Blount,
Joe Register, J. Philip Hogan, Loren Triplett

STAR building 1983
30x50 office area on left, 50x50x20 studio on right

STAR staff and part-time volunteers

We thought we would never outgrow these facilities, but by the end of 1984 we needed even more offices, because the 30x50 building became crowded with prop storage, control room, the make-up area, duplication machines, and shipping counters.

Jim Reis, vice-president of a manufactured-homes company, custom designed a double-wide for us—with a small kitchen, conference room, lobby, and six offices. We parked the "office" beside the studio building.

Meanwhile, Red processed hundreds of orders for both radio and video programs. One order came from missionary Frank Burns. He told us that he and his wife, Doris, had tried to begin a church in Torreón, Mexico. They did all the usual things to plant a church—they rented a facility, advertised, and prayed; and then they sang and preached as hard as they could night after night.

But, for some reason, they just couldn't get more than about forty people to come out to the services. The weather was cold and rainy. It even snowed! And who wants to come out in that kind of weather? But one day, Frank had an idea; he sensed that it was the Lord impressing him, "Why not show *Lugar Secreto*?" He had a VCR, a TV, and some videotapes.

So that very night, he set up the equipment and played a thirty-minute program. People gathered around to watch; they seemed to enjoy it. "Tomorrow night I'll show another program," Frank said. "Come back and bring your friends."

They did! Night after night the crowd grew ... 50, 100, 300, and then, over 500!

Frank asked us, "Have you ever seen 300 children gathered around a thirteen-inch screen? You should see it! They laugh and sing along and pray with Cristina and Bobo. We gave each child a Bible story coloring book, the one that is mentioned on the program. And every night our daughter, Wylene, taught the corresponding story. You should have seen the way the children took care of those books! They covered them with brightly colored paper, and some even asked older cousins or brothers or sisters to color the pictures so they would be perfect."

Wylene encouraged the children to tell others about what they were learning. One night a child came, leading by the hand a ninety-year-old man. The child had talked to the elderly man about Jesus and had prayed with him.

Frank continued, "Finally, we separated the children from the adults. Some of the adults weren't very happy at first—they didn't want to miss their favorite TV show!"

These new converts began to ask Frank to take the program to their neighborhoods on Saturdays. Subsequently, they opened fifty outstations, five of which became churches.

And the children's prison! "Would you believe they let us into the prison?" Frank asked. "These are not kids caught in petty theft—these are street kids: murderers at eight and ten and twelve years of age. Every week we went into the prison to show *Lugar Secreto* and give away the Bible story books. The guards do not allow preaching in the prison, but they love the television programs!"

Frank continued, "Doris and I want to begin a new church in another area of Mexico. This time, we want to begin with *Lugar Secreto*. Sure, it's hard to lug around the VCR and the television set. It's a lot of trouble. But ... then, I watch those faces: a child, an old lady, a young man. People captivated by the puppets, by the humor, and caught by the presence of God. Believe me, it is worth all the bother. I thank God for *Lugar Secreto*."

***

Stories of the results of our programs sustained us even though raising the money for all the needs at STAR proved to be a constant challenge. Boys and Girls Missionary Crusade (BGMC) gave funds for video tapes; and Light for the Lost (LFTL) men's ministries donated thousands of dollars for printed materials; and Speed the Light (STL) youth groups bought tens of thousands of dollars' worth of equipment for the ministry. But, for operating expenses, we continued to visit churches. Peninsular Florida District, as I've mentioned, opened wide its doors to us and we visited almost every church. The pastors welcomed us, hosted us to good restaurants and comfortable hotels. The church people gave generous offerings. Joe and I traveled to West Florida and also to West Virginia, where Superintendent Irving Steiding opened the district to us. Maxine, his wife, invited me to tour the District with them and to speak to Women's Ministries groups and girls' retreats.

***

Who could have ever dreamed when Fredda Marsh donated four little puppets to us in 1977 that such a world-wide ministry would result? Several times through the years, Fredda traveled to STAR to visit us and be with "her children" during our productions. Of course, she wanted each of her puppets to look its very best for the shoot. However, we wanted the puppet to be dressed according to the script—sometimes with his hair messed up, or his shoes scuffed, or with dirt on his knee. But Fredda would wait until we were distracted, then she'd grab a puppet and style his hair. She carried a hairbrush and hairspray. If his tummy-foam had slipped sideways or slid too far down, "Mama" would grab that puppet, turn him inside out, and twist his insides around. I was shocked! We always treated the puppets so delicately for fear of "hurting" them in some way.

Fredda always came equipped with her hot-glue gun and needle and thread. She would stretch her hand up inside a puppet's head to replace or reposition the foam in the cheeks and jaw. When she created the Mary Magdalene puppet, Fredda sewed pink lace on the inside, where no one could see, but she wanted her to feel special!

Fredda actually starred in one of our videos, *How to Make Puppets*. Toni, a mischievous, little kid puppet Fredda had made, sat beside her, pestering her with questions, "Is that how you made my arm, Mama? When you made my fingers did you stick a finger up my nose? I remember when you poked that stuffing in my leg. It hurt-ed me. I cried 'ouchy-ouchy-ouchy,' but you just kept right on sewing me together."

Fredda in the puppet room

***

As ministry opportunities continued to open throughout Latin America, Red needed more and more copies of tapes. That's when God sent Ed Bissonnette, retired aviation mechanic, to take over the duplication area. Suffering with arthritis in his knees and ankles, Ed scooted around from machine to machine on a wheeled stool.

Ed soon established "his domain" and was grouchy if anyone so much as looked sideways at *his* machines! We all steered clear of his area and let him work to his heart's content. I wonder how many thousands of programs he duplicated? And how many thousands of lives Ed touched?

A Place for People, Puppets, and Cockroach Soup

LUGAR SECRETO 1987

audio/ mikes and monitors
ROLAND BLOUNT
LARRY KILLION

bookkeeper/receptionist
GERRI JACKSON

cameramen
DARA BRANNAN
EVELYN BLOUNT
FRANCINE KILLION
SANDRA BASS
STEVE GRANER

construction
GERALD JACKSON
TROY KLOEFKORN
TOM TRUMBO

cooks
HILDA SWINDAL
MARY TRUMBO

devotions
STEVE GRANER

director/associates
JOE REGISTER
ANDY SHETLEY
DARA BRANNAN

engineer
CAROL YOUNG

floor director/log
MARAGARET REGISTER
SANDRA BASS

lighting
CAROL YOUNG
ANDY SHETLEY

make up
FRANCINE KILLION

quality control
JOE REGISTER

office
NEIL RUDA
CARL HULTGREN
HAROLD MINTLE
RED DEAN

photography
FRANCINE KILLION

props (small)
GERRY HULTGREN

puppet caretakers
CRISTIANA PORTER
MARITZA SEGURA
SARITA SEGURA

puppeteer coordinator
JUDY GRANER

set dressing
SANDRA BASS
DARA BRANNAN
CAROL COLEMAN
FRANCINE KILLION

sets/ setup & tear down
CAROL YOUNG
FRANCINE KILLION
CAROL COLEMAN
DARA BRANNAN
CARLOS LUNA

teleprompter
BEA MINTLE
CARLOS LUNA

video monitors
CAROL YOUNG
DARA BRANNAN
ANDY SHETLEY

warehouse
CAROL YOUNG

WORLDWIDE DUPLICATION
ED BISSIONNETTE
BEA MINTLE
DAVE & SHIRLEY INGLIS

Lugar Secreto Crew List, May 1987

"I BEAT MY DRUMS FOR JESUS."
"TOCO MI TAMBOR PARA CRISTO."

21

Tim

I should have known!

1983 – 1988

    Tim stood tall in the red robe and mortarboard. He flipped the tassel with a triumphant grin. He was graduated from Kathleen High School. Band buddies Ruel, Joey, and Greg gathered around vowing to maintain friendships, no matter what. Time now for Tim to hang up his trombone and Drum Major uniform and get ready to travel to Evangel College, where he hoped to receive academic credit for all the video production skills he had practiced and honed since he was fourteen years old.

    I remembered the day, five years earlier, when Timmy and I had been driving home from church. He said, emphatically, his voice popping with deepening tones, "Mom, please call me Tim. I am not 'Timmy' any longer." I agreed, and he continued, "Can we stop at McDonald's?" "Sorry, we don't have the money, *Tim*."

    Tim thought for a moment before asking, "Are we poor?" I had not thought about it. Our budget was tight. Very tight. In fact, a pastor from the Main Street church had called and said that someone would pay tuition for the kids to attend the church school, but we would need to pay for the bus—$100 per month per child. We did not have it. The kids could not attend. But poor? Haltingly, I answered, "I don't think so, Tim. You know that Women's Ministries groups gave us our towels and sheets and dishes. We have money to pay the expenses of the house and car every month. And enough money for groceries, if I'm careful to make everything 'from scratch,' and don't buy prepared foods. But ... we certainly don't have any money left over."

***

Tim loved video production and seemed to be a natural at every aspect of it. At home he would take things apart to see how they worked, and when I vacuumed his room, all sorts of sounds clinked their way up the vacuum cleaner hose. At the studio, he produced the Bible verse segments. He wrote the script, drew the storyboard, lit and decorated the set, ran the audio, shot, and edited. He became carpenter and puppet-master, building sets and sewing things onto the puppets' hands. He produced these segments throughout his high school years, varying the style of shooting for every series. One year, he even used "claymation," spending hours with the clay figures, which moved only a fraction of an inch "frame by frame."

On one occasion, Tim called Joe to see a rough-cut segment. The video showed a puppet standing at the roadside thumbing a ride. Tim had shot a close-up of the puppet's hand, thumb extended. He had shot the puppet's head turning from side to side looking for a ride. Tim had stood beside the puppet with the camera to get the puppet's POV (point of view) as a car approached. Then, the camera swirled, and all of a sudden, the puppet lay sprawled on the highway, obviously hit by the car.

Joe admired Tim's handiwork, the excellent storyline, the sequencing of events. But, he was sorry to tell Tim that the scene was just a little too violent for *Lugar Secreto*.

One day, working alone in the studio, Tim climbed the 15-foot ladder to adjust a light hanging from the light grid 17 feet above the floor. Suddenly, the ladder slipped out from under him. He reached up and grabbed onto the grid. It held his weight. He stretched his leg toward the ladder. His toes barely touched the side. He swung his leg, hooked the toe of his shoe around the side, and tugged. He swung and tugged again and again, and finally brought the ladder close enough to climb back onto it.

Another day, using the hot-glue gun, Tim cried out "Ayi, no!" Joe looked at Tim's hand and burst out laughing. He couldn't help it. Tim's thumb and a finger were hot-glued together.

Tim on the ladder, fifteen feet in the air

***

Someone had given us a "second car." It was a huge, old, gold, gas-guzzler "tank," and the kids, ashamed of it, made me let them off a block away from any event. The turning radius was so large that turning a corner took a lot of thought. One day Tim came into the house, "Dad, have you seen the car the neighbors have for sale? It's a decent one! Can we buy it, please?"

Joe said if Tim would go talk to the neighbors and negotiate a price, we would consider it. A few minutes later, Tim came home grinning from ear to ear, "They will trade their AMC Pacer for our old clunker. We just have to assume their payments—we'll save that much on gasoline. They only owe a little bit …." Sure enough, we traded for that silver Pacer with red interior, and we ran that car until it died of old age. The roof liner sagged and fell onto our heads. We tore it off, and then foam shredded into our hair. We always had to brush off when we got out of the car.

Tim recruited his buddy, Joe O'Brien, to help run camera for a shoot. Acting silly, they tussled in the hallway and knocked a hole in our new drywall … but Joey became a great cameraman and went on to become a videographer, making television and movie production his career.

One summer, Randy Gould came to stay with us and help at STAR. He and Tim were friends, growing up as fellow MKs in Paraguay. The two teens drove the Pacer in front of us on the way to the studio. We traveled parallel to a railroad track, and then turned left, across the tracks onto another road.

At the intersection there was a traffic light. The light turned yellow as Tim approached. He turned the corner just in time, prepared to sail across the railroad tracks. However, none of us had noticed a train traveling at exactly our speed, zooming along the tracks beside us, only slightly behind us. As Tim's car crossed the tracks, he saw the train headlight—huge—in his left peripheral vision and hit the gas pedal. Tim and Randy whooshed over the tracks *inches* in front of the train. It was one of the most frightening moments of our lives. There were no gates or warning lights at the railroad crossing. Since then, gates have been installed.

***

Crysti had moved away from home to the Southeastern College campus. She had already changed her name from Christy to Crysti, and by her second year of college, she was ready to change her last name, too—to Porter. To complete a college credit, Crysti was assigned to a children's church in Plant City. The requirement was to attend there once a week. But I noticed that she volunteered to attend on Sunday evenings and Wednesday nights, too. Hmmm ... Douglas Porter also attended those services.

Doug was perfect for Crysti. Almost all of the college guys she had dated were intimidated by her being on television, having lived abroad, speaking another language. But not Doug. He had already begun his career with the Tampa International Airport, where he continues to work with USAirways. Doug is confident of who he is. Instead of being threatened, he seemed fulfilled by Crysti's gregarious spirit.

As I write this, they have been married for thirty years and Doug continues to be patient, supportive, and loving, with a true servant's heart.

Doug, Crysti, Joe, Margaret, Jennifer, Tim
Family Photo 1983

Another "Kris," Kristine, met Tim at Evangel College. Tim called to say he was bringing Kris home for Thanksgiving to meet us. By now Crysti and Doug were married and had a baby, Jennifer. They came to our house, and we were all sitting around waiting for Tim and Kris to arrive.

Suddenly, Crysti said, "Hey, let's dress up! Let's play a joke on Tim. We'll look as tacky as we can!"

We scurried to find ugly, ill-fitting clothes. Joe blacked out a front tooth. He pulled a camouflage hat down to his ears. He put on an embroidered dress shirt from Paraguay, and stuffed a pillow inside for a big belly. He put on a striped necktie and tied it very long. He wore shorts, with loafers and black socks. Crysti pulled a bra strap down onto her arm, mis-buttoned her blouse, messed up her hair and tied a scarf around her neck. She dressed baby Jennifer in a droopy diaper and smudged her face. Doug put on an old pair of Tim's jeans—high waters, with black socks and brown dress shoes. He found a ball cap and a too-small knit shirt and a too-short necktie. I put on an old dress from Paraguay, sloppy and baggy, and wore Joe's old work-boots with long black socks.

The car pulled up the driveway. We knew we could not open the front door ... because if Tim saw us, he would just keep on driving, offering Kris some excuse. We waited. We heard footsteps on the porch, the front door opened. We all drawled, "Howdy, Krees. Welcum ta tha Reg-stir how-ouse."

Tim groaned, "I should have known! I should have warned her!"

Kris just stood staring at us, her mouth dropped open.

I don't know why Kris didn't want to be part of our family ... she and Tim soon ended their relationship. Funny how things like that just happen, for no reason.

Family welcoming party

Tim double majored in Communications and Drama and, by the time he graduated from Evangel College, he had directed many segments of *Lugar Secreto* during his summer and winter breaks. He made Bobo fly through the air on a Tarzan-vine-swing; ride a bicycle; and float past the scene on a sailboat.

Plus, Tim directed our first Spanish educational series for International Correspondence Institute (ICI, now Global University). ICI sent over from Belgium a director to be certain that we shot everything correctly. Christopher Garnold-Smith sat in the studio, arms crossed, legs crossed, to see what we could do. Gradually, his legs uncrossed, his arms uncrossed, he shook his head and exclaimed, "You don't need me!" Tim just grinned, looking the part of the confident director in his jeans, white shirt and blue blazer.

Tim has developed into an excellent award-winning producer, director, and videographer, making video production his profession.

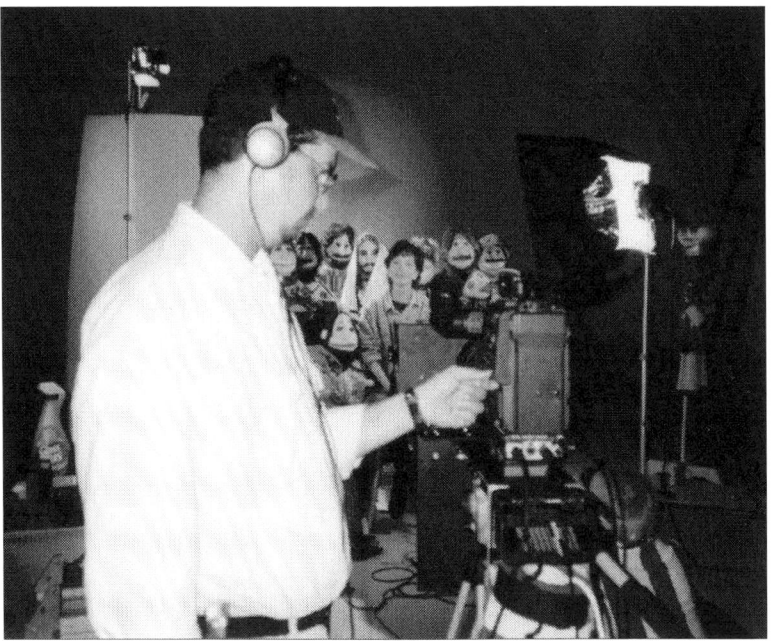

Tim readying the camera for a shoot

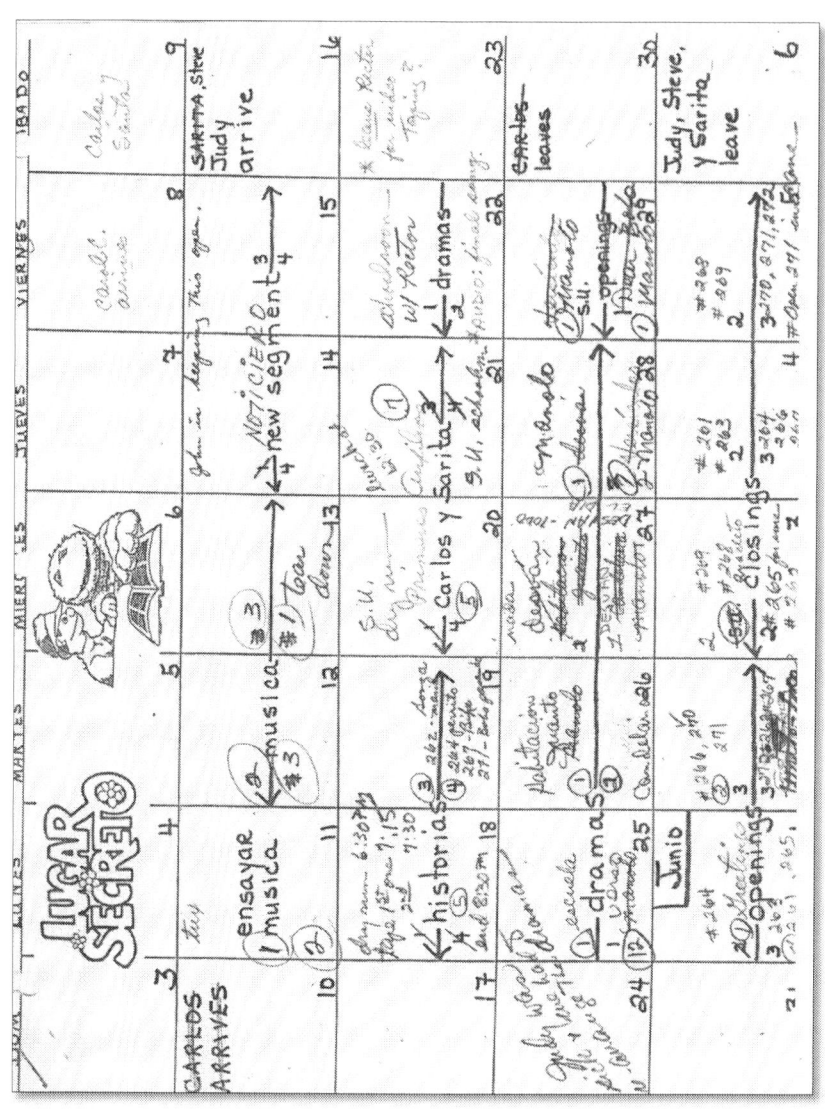

Lugar Secreto shooting calendar May 1987

Dear BoBo
I watch your show every day,
I Like the show you had on
good hugs and bad hugs,
It helped me to understand
Thing my nana has been
talking to me about, how
some people can be very bad,
and I am Learning a lot about
Jesus, and one day I will
Fully understand all about asking
Jesus to be my Savior,
    I Love you all
    and I will keep on watching
    every day.
my name is Candi~
I am six years old
I Live in C
★ 100 ~~Cotton~~ street (OVER)
Collins ~~cotton~~ ~~29607~~

A Place for People, Puppets, and Cockroach Soup

"CAN YOU GUESS WHAT I HAVE TO SHARE?"
"¿PUEDES ADIVINAR LO QUE YO PUEDO COMPARTIR?"

22

Toni

Who-meeee?

People who have never had a place for puppets in their lives have no concept of the intense, very real personalities that each puppet can develop. Once when we were brainstorming a segment, Joe suggested that a specific puppet could play a new role. Shocked, the puppeteer replied, "No! He would never do that!" Another time, Jero Pérez operated a young-man-puppet in a drama and when we finished, Jero asked, "On the next series, could he break up with this girl?—he doesn't like her."

The summer of 1981, when we shot at the Southeastern College campus, two of Sarita's scripts called for a baby boy, old enough to talk. In a box of "extra puppets" from Fredda lay a smallish, dark brown puppet that we had never used. We had avoided using him because he was not very pretty—his nose seemed too big, his head seemed too small, his black hair lay plastered flat against his head. He had dangling, skinny arms and no legs. Crysti and Maritza held him up and tried to imagine him as a baby boy. "Let's go to Goodwill and Salvation Army. Maybe we can find some baby clothes," Crysti said. "And a hat to cover his pitiful head," sighed Maritza.

So, along with Sarita and Judy, they went shopping. They came back with a baby blanket, a yellow bonnet, a baby's tee shirt, and a pacifier. They dressed the new kid in his used clothes and glued the pacifier to his hand. In the scripts, his name was Toñito; he was precocious and witty.

In the first puppet script, Marta, big sister to Toñito, lay in a hammock, peacefully resting. Then Momma told Marta to baby-sit while Momma ran to the store. Toñito sat in the grass beside the hammock. His no-legs were swaddled in a blanket. Hindered not in the least, Toñito pestered and pestered and pestered poor Marta, who had picked up her Bible and was trying to memorize her Bible verse for the week. Totally exasperated, Marta suddenly reached out of the hammock, grabbed Toñito's hand with the pacifier and stuffed it down his throat. Toñito grunted and spit and hollered and cried. Looking at her Bible verse again, Marta realized it was about patience ... and so, she repented, and comforted Toñito.

In the second script, puppet Dad, just home from work, sat on the couch while he tried to relax and read the newspaper. Toñito sat beside him, his no-legs again swaddled in his used baby blanket. All of a sudden, Toñito's pacifier arm swings against the newspaper. *"Papi. Papi. ¡¡¡PAAPIIITOOO!!!"* (Daddy. Daddy. DAADDDY!)

"¿Qué, Toñito?" (What, Toni?)

"¿Sabes qué?" (Ya know what?)

"¿Qué?" (What?)

"Naaadaa...." (Nothin'....)

Dad straightens the newspaper, continues reading. Ker-blam! *"Papi, Papi. ¡¡¡PAAPIIITOOO!!!"* And again, and again!

I don't remember the object of that particular drama, but that first day, we all laughed so much at Toni that we knew he needed to be a "regular," and that meant he needed legs. So we called Fredda, who said, "Of course, I'll make him some legs. But I don't remember which fabric I used for him. Send him to me, and I will try to match the fabric."

A few weeks later, Toni came "home" with his long, skinny arms and his new, long, skinny legs. Fredda had found a boys' red jumper, a white shirt, white socks, and some little red and white tennis shoes.

Sarita had no idea what her script and Crysti's puppeteering skills would create! Sarita calls it *"chispa y ternura"* (spark-flying-humor combined with tenderness). Even now, thirty years later, Toni, still a baby, has entranced tens of thousands of televiewers and has interviewed hundreds of pastors—much to their chagrin (and their delight)!

Crysti and Toni

Fredda persuaded Pastor Dan Betzer to come to STAR to sing some of his recorded songs with the puppets. Dan, very hesitantly, told us he could stop by on his way home from Belgium and sing a couple of songs. We paired Dan with Toni. On the set, Dan spoke a few words to Toni and then began to sing his first song. Toni joined in the chorus—deliberately way off key! Dan smiled. Just before the second song, on camera, Dan ad-libbed with Toni. Nonchalantly, Toni asked, "Brother Dan, do you ever get Oreo cookie crumbs in your belly button?" Shocked, Dan grinned, "Cookie crumbs in my belly button?" "Yeah, you know, when you eat Oreo cookies in bed and some of those crumbs..." Dan laughed and said something like, "Uh, I think we'd better start this song."

I thought I would die of embarrassment. As soon as the song ended, I apologized to Dan. He started laughing, "No, I love it. Let's do another song." We taped all day long, recording every song that Dan had with him. And as Dan and Toni ad-libbed, they formed a special bond across that unique bridge of rare, comedic timing.

Sometime later, Roland said, "Crysti, I need to record Toni in the sound booth." Every year we produced a promotional video, and

Toni needed to sing his line of "Somebody Has to Tell the World about Jesus."

(I need to explain here that ever since our days together as missionaries in Paraguay, Crysti always used the missionary-kid-title for adult missionaries of "Aunt and Uncle.")

So Crysti settled before the microphone, and called, "OK, Uncle Roland, I'm ready." Roland played the music track, and Crysti began to sing, but she couldn't get Toni's voice to sound "right."

"Hold on, Uncle Roland, I've got to run and get Toni. I can't do his voice unless he's on my hand." When Crysti returned with Toni, she couldn't adjust the microphone because one hand held Toni and the other hand held the words to the song. "Just a second," Evelyn volunteered, "I'll help." Evelyn adjusted the mike, and Toni began to sing his line.

"Uh. Something's still not right," Roland announced. "Let's try it one more time."

They tried it once more, and again, the sound was not good. Roland said, "It sounds terrible—there is no 'presence'—it's like the mike is too far away." Being blind, he couldn't see what the problem might be.

Crysti began to laugh, "Uncle Roland, it's because Aunt Evelyn did not place the mike in front of *me*—she is holding the mike in front of Toni!"

Toni, bilingual, could appear in both *Lugar Secreto* and *Secret Place*. So could puppets operated by Judy and her new husband, Steve Graner, and by missionaries Charles and Linda Stewart, and by John Taylor.

Our English-only puppeteers included Shelby and Connie Lanier and Jenny Penhallegon. Rita Christy interacted with Toni on many *Secret Place* programs, and, of course, so did Dan Betzer.

Whenever the puppeteers gathered to shoot more shows, they always brought back stories of children and adults who watched *Lugar Secreto*. John Taylor told us about one time in Honduras when he traveled to a tiny village high up in the mountains. John had told his new friends there that he couldn't stay very many days because he needed to return to STAR to tape more *Lugar Secreto* programs.

"¡*Lugar Secreto!*" they exclaimed, "our favorite show!"

A Place for People, Puppets, and Cockroach Soup

"It can't be. You don't have TVs; you don't even have electricity in the village."

"*No importa*," they replied. "Every month, a man climbs the mountain with his burro carrying a TV, VCR, and generator."

John began to do some of the character voices. "*Gonzalo el Malo*," they cried; then, "*¡Abuelo!*" (Grandpa!)

John's *Abuelo* character would sing in a high falsetto and hold out his notes long and loud. One day on the Honduran Mesquito Coast, John walked past a thatched roof hut and heard Grandpa's falsetto. John peeped inside to see a crowd of children and adults sitting on a dirt floor in front of a television set. A cable ran across the dirt floor, under the wood-slatted wall, to a generator behind the hut. The TV screen sparkled with *Lugar Secreto*.

Watching *Lugar Secreto*

Coming from Colombia, Charles and Linda Stewart brought with them a young man, Carlos Luna, who worked with them in children's ministry. After Carlos' first series, we could not imagine a *Lugar Secreto* without him. The next year a young lady also accompanied them, Amanda, soon to be Carlos' wife.

For several years, Carlos and Sarita, as "live people," did a mad scientist segment with Toni. Sarita carried Toni onto the set in her arms, with one arm stretched up inside Toni to make him "real." Then the camera focused on Mad Scientist Carlos while Sarita placed Toni on a lab-table and Crysti took over the puppeteering from underneath the table. Toni could begin talking even before Crysti was fully situated with the puppet, because the camera was not focused on him.

Sarita, Toni, and Carlos in his Mad Scientist costume

Carlos also worked "live" as a singer in an outdoor restaurant. Missionary Larry Killion arranged and performed the background music for him. We even found an old piano that Larry, as a puppet, "played" on set.

***

Puppeteering is hard work. Arms, hands, wrists, shoulders, neck, head, back, legs, knees, feet—everything aches from being stretched and twisted and immobilized in awkward positions for hours on end. Aunt Gerry Hultgren, hostess to the puppeteers, scurried from station to station with pillows, pieces of foam, water, safety pins, highlighter pens, tape, scissors, needle and thread, puppet-rods for the arms and tie-wraps to hold the rods in place, and anything else that could possibly alleviate the pain and suffering. Especially popular was the big bottle of Tylenol! Oh, and Aunt

A Place for People, Puppets, and Cockroach Soup

Gerry made sure that everyone wore one of the famous black cloth "hoods" we had designed to cover puppeteers' arms and hair just in case they were in the shot.

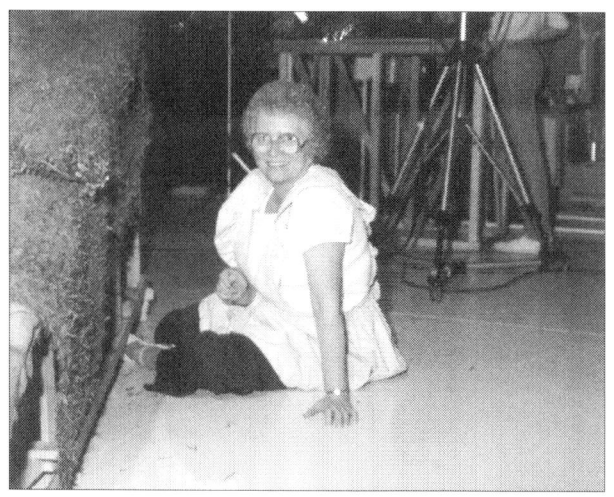

Aunt Gerry ready to help puppeteers under the set

One year a new person joined us. I'll call her Fanny. Well, Fanny worked diligently her very first day as puppeteer. Although complaining as she went, nevertheless, she did an excellent job. The next morning she appeared with both arms wrapped from shoulders to tips of fingers in Ace bandages. We didn't dare laugh!

The following day as we developed a drama-script, Sarita made some adjustments to the main character's script to make her be a hypochondriac. It was all in Spanish, of course, which Fanny did not understand, and it was done in playful humor, not maliciously. Did we ever have fun with that puppet's aches and pains!

Then, the following week, Fanny "ran camera" and, believe me, she came prepared. Our cameras were old and the video would "smear" when we panned or zoomed if an object was extremely bright. So, to apply a matte finish to a shiny object, we used dulling spray frequently and abundantly. On that particular day, when I reached for the dulling spray can, Fanny grabbed for a bag she had brought, stuck her hand inside, and pulled out an antique, green, World War II gas mask. She flung it on her head, with its bug eyes and snout protruding. Her breath sounded like Darth Vader. How we kept our composure and contained our laughter until we were out of the room, I do not know.

***

By now we had solved one of our greatest obstacles: helping the puppeteers to see what their puppet was doing. With the puppet high up in the air, or on top of a set, the puppeteer could not see exactly where the puppet's eyes looked. The puppet needed to "look at," to "follow" the action. So, we learned to use video monitors down under the set, enabling the puppeteers to "see" what their puppets "did." But the image in the monitor is reversed, so, at first, the puppeteer would move his puppet in the opposite direction, causing laughs and re-takes. The monitors needed to be tilted at crazy angles, depending on how twisted a stance the puppeteer was in. So, Joe and the crew built wooden brackets with dowels to prop up the monitors.

***

Every *Secret Place* and *Lugar Secreto* program consists of short segments: the opening-greeting, an object lesson, the Bible verse (usually with puppets), the Bible story (with Judy in Spanish; Ginger Brown or me in English), music, a puppet drama, closing prayer, and a song.

Without a doubt, the most challenging segments to shoot were the drama segments. Through the years, we developed a "Sequence of Set-up" for them. First, we chose the general theme for the entire 13 or 26 shows we would shoot. Then, the specific themes for each show. For example: *Bible Heroes; Daniel*. During the months of pre-production, Sarita wrote the drama scripts to depict real-life applications. Some characters she knew well, and she could flesh out their lines. Other characters would be new, and each puppeteer would contribute to the actual lines spoken.

So, when we assembled for a month-long shoot, the next step was to meet in the conference room for a "read-through" in puppet voices and personalities. The puppeteers would laugh, ad lib, and flesh out the drama. Then they would split up—some to gather the props and costumes needed, some to dress the puppets for the segment, and others to set up the puppet platforms.

We would block (move the puppets on the set according to the script), place the furniture, then stand or "sit" the puppets in place, and light the set. After that, we would decorate the set with strewn toys or plants or pictures or whatever props we needed. And finally we would place the audio and video monitors down underneath the platforms and run the audio and video cables. To reach the 17-foot-high lighting grid, we used the very heavy, 15-foot ladder, on castors, and it couldn't travel over the cables, so we had to have the lighting correct before we ran the cables.

Once the puppeteers took their places, we would adjust monitors, then try to make each puppeteer as comfortable as the tiny spaces would allow. Sometimes, we would spend hours setting up for a 3-minute drama. In fact, we calculated that *each minute* of an edited show consumed 300 hours, including the pre-production, production, and post-production.

***

For years Judy wanted to design and draw a coloring book of the *Lugar Secreto—Secret Place* cast as our giveaway. Finally, thanks to the printing costs being covered by donations from *Light for the Lost (*LFTL, men's ministries) and *Boys and Girls Missionary Crusade* (BGMC), we held in our hands a professional, bilingual, bright yellow, 8x10 coloring book! Bobo and Toni and Rosita and Tomasito fill the pages, along with other puppets, and Bible verses and a beautiful prayer in both English and Spanish. (Some of those pages are copied in this book.)

In every show, when we offered the book, we never stated an address. The puppets simply said, "Write to the address on the screen." This allowed missionaries in each country to place their address on the screen and to do follow-up on the write-ins. So, everywhere, children believed that Bobo lived in *their* country, and they would mail pictures and objects to him—such as the cockroaches he was always cooking and eating....

In one of our video segments, Toni sits in his high chair with a crayon in one hand. He colors furiously in his coloring book and waves his pacifier with his other hand. He looks up at the viewer. "You want one of these coloring books with my picture? You can have one. And you know how much it costs? *Nada. Nada. Nada. Es gratis.*" (Nothin', nothin', nothin'. It's free.)

And it *was* free, paid for by donors; and by the hard work of many volunteers and missionaries; and by the blood, sweat, tears, and laughter … and the pain of puppeteers.

***

After showing *Lugar Secreto* in Colombia, missionary Myrna Wilkins prays with children.

Dear BoBo

I recieved your coloring Book and was very happy To Hear from you. I like your program alot. I want you to put my father in prayer so That God can Help Him stop drinking. He saids He wants To quiet But does not know How He saids He is Tired of drinking please pray for Him I like your Bible storys. To I Learn a LaT from All of your Firends BoBo me und my sister like your program.

By Eugene   I am 8 years old.

"LET US LOVE (AND HELP) ONE ANOTHER."
"AMEMONOS (Y AYUDEMONOS) UNOS A OTROS."

23

Dottie and Ken

Hold your breath, please.

1985—

The elderly woman bounced over to Joe. "Brother Joe, I want to help you in your TV ministry!"

Joe looked down into twinkling eyes set in wrinkled skin bronzed by 70 years of sunshine. He and the woman were standing to the left side of the platform in the little chapel at Carpenter's Home Church in Lakeland, Florida.

Joe and I loved to attend the Sunday school class held there, and this morning our teacher, Dr. Edgar Lee, had given Joe a few moments to make an appeal for help at STAR.

As soon as the class dismissed, the woman hurried over to Joe. "What can I do?" she asked again.

"Well, what do you know *how* to do?" Joe questioned.

"Apply make-up."

"Great! We will need a make-up artist for our next production in two weeks."

"Just one thing," the woman said more slowly, her eyes twinkling merrily. "Ah ... the people will need to hold their breath—when I apply the make-up. And ... lie down."

Baffled, Joe stared into her dancing eyes.

"I only know how to put make-up on dead people! I worked at a funeral home."

She and Joe nearly *died* laughing (pardon the pun).

"Oh, yeah," the woman continued, gasping for breath, "And also, I can only fix the front of someone's hair. I've never had to style anyone's hair in the back!"

That is how Dottie and Ken Williams, married for many years, integrated into the STAR family as if they'd been there forever.

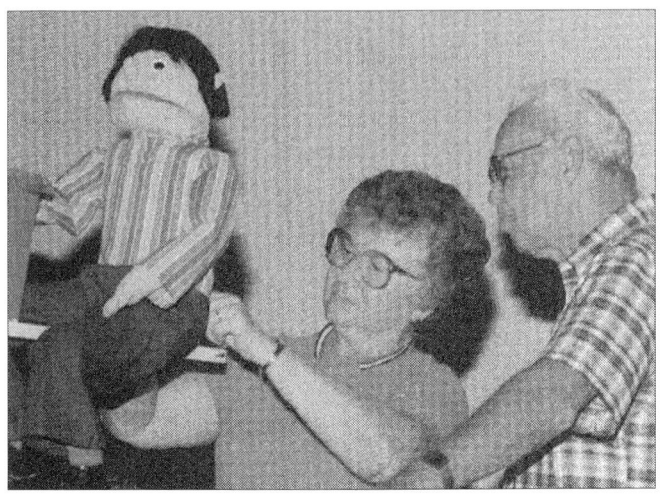

Dottie and Ken Williams

Dottie designed the make-up station, bought mirrors, shopped for make-up in various shades of colors, and found a red and white polka dot cape to cover her clients' "bodies" so make-up would not soil their clothes.

"Hey, Dottie," I told her, "Next month Bernhard Johnson is bringing a team to shoot a series of shows for broadcast in Brazil. His associate, Bruce Braithwaite, says they will bring about a dozen people, and I'm assuming they'll be all shades—from white to brown to black."

"No problem," Dottie smiled. "How do you say 'hold your breath' in Portuguese?"

One by one the Brazilians traipsed to Dottie's station: white missionaries, a brown male soloist, a browner violinist, some creamy brown vocalists, a deep black guitarist. Eliel, Ceil, Seraphim, Carlos, Vitorino, Misael, Doris, and Beth.

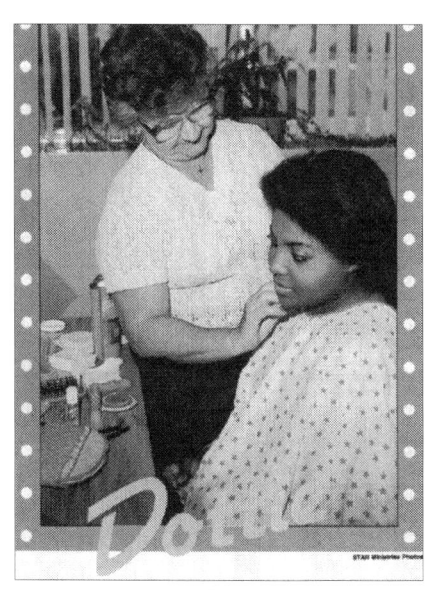

Dottie at her station,
featured in *Mountain Movers* magazine, August 1986

Dottie learned each person's name, often mispronouncing it atrociously. She could put at ease the most nervous talent. By the time the beautifully-made-up person left her station, he or she would be all smiles and ready to begin the shoot. Dottie did more than apply make-up, she applied love. "At 70," she laughed with a twinkle in her eye, "I can hug and pat shoulders, and they know I'm not flirting. I'm just loving them."

"What!?" Dottie gasped, a few minutes later, as she stood at the edge of the studio to watch the male soloist, Vitorino, begin to tape his first song. "He has two arms!"

"Yeah," I replied.

"But, he doesn't!" Dottie exclaimed in a loud whisper. "He had only one arm when I made him up earlier!"

She was right. Vitorino's artificial arm was cumbersome and he wore it only when he was on stage!

I was floor director, so when Vitorino finished his song, I said in a loud voice, in Spanish, "*Corte* (Cut). *Muy bien hecho, hermano* (Very good job, brother)." And in exaggerated style, I made the universal signal for OK by forming an "O" with my thumb and forefinger while holding up three fingers. Vitorino looked startled,

A Place for People, Puppets, and Cockroach Soup

and averted his eyes quickly. Of course he spoke Portuguese and I spoke Spanish, but I had assumed he would understand "*muy bien*" and if not that, at least my hand-sign of "good job." Undeterred by his ingratitude, I motioned for the next musicians to take their places on the set.

Once again, when they finished their song, I congratulated them and gave them an enthusiastic hand signal of "OK." Once again, they looked startled and quickly looked away. "Good grief," I thought, "these Brazilians sure don't accept praise very well."

The practice continued all day long, song after song, musician after musician. Finally at the close of the day, Eliel, who spoke a little Spanish, approached me. "*Hermana Margarita* (Sister Margaret)," he began slowly, "Thank you for complimenting us today … but do you have to make that obscene gesture with your hand?"

"What!? This sign?" I quickly formed the OK sign and gave it to him. He jerked and looked away.

"Yes! That sign! In Brazil it is … how do you say … it is like giving someone 'the finger.'"

Mortified, I stammered, "Oh, no! What can I do instead?"

Eliel smiled, and closing his fist as he extended his thumb, he gave me a firm "thumbs up"!

At the close of the second day, Joe asked to talk to Bernhard privately. "How are we doing? Are you pleased? What should we do differently?"

Bernhard shook his head, "Joe, we've never had a production flow so smoothly. Your technical crew makes my people look good on camera. When you told me that there would be no charge for this series, just the actual expenses, I thought there was some 'catch to it,' but now, we see your sincerity. When can we come back?"

Once or twice a year for many years, the Bernhard Johnson team came to shoot a new series of programs. Their *Christmas Special* even won an *Angel Award!*

Later, Bernhard wrote to us, "How can we ever thank you for everything you did for us during our time there? It was just great working with you, and everyone felt that way. We so appreciated the facilities, the relaxed atmosphere, and the many kindnesses. The Brazilian guys really enjoyed being there and getting acquainted with all of you. We look forward to working together again."

A Place for People, Puppets, and Cockroach Soup

On the set of *Bernhard Johnson Presents*
Bernhard, seated, on right

Joe, Bernhard Johnson, and Bruce Braithwaite
hold the Silver Angel trophy.

***

Day after day, month after month, we had hardly noticed quiet Ken, Dottie's husband. Nevertheless, we felt the effects of Ken's presence. He helped behind the scenes, quickly available to move a set-piece or re-route a cable.

Like a quiet shadow, as we readied the studio and control room for a shoot, Ken would walk the perimeter of the studio floor. He skirted the flats, glided behind the scenery, and touched gently the pieces of the set. He strolled slowly past the grand piano where Doris Johnson rehearsed. He softly circled the corner where the guitarist practiced, fingering chords on his gleaming Brazilian guitar. Ken moved into the control room, striding silently behind the crew and stood unobtrusively beside the equipment.

Step after step, day after day, Ken moved his lips without a sound as he interceded for God to bless each production, each crew member, each performer, and each televiewer.

Dear Secret Place Staff,

Let me say to you how much I enjoy your program! Right from the time you begin the show on thru to the end I am glued to the T.V. screen. (I must tell you I am only 32 yrs. old & I love it!) ☺

I work with our Jr. Church & we also have a puppet ministry we have just started. One day a week I volunteer at our Day Care where I have a puppet skit. Your show has helped me a lot! If I had to say what my favorite thing is — I couldn't say. I just love Bo-Bo & the school classroom & Captain Allen & the Bible story & all the singing & Cricki & Buster & Tony. All of it is truly wonderful. We have started taping the shows. What could be better than watching 2 hrs. of Secret Place on a rainy afternoon or a friday night or after school one afternoon or to share w/ others.?

I thank God for your devotion & your love & concern for other souls. May God richly bless you all & your

(over)

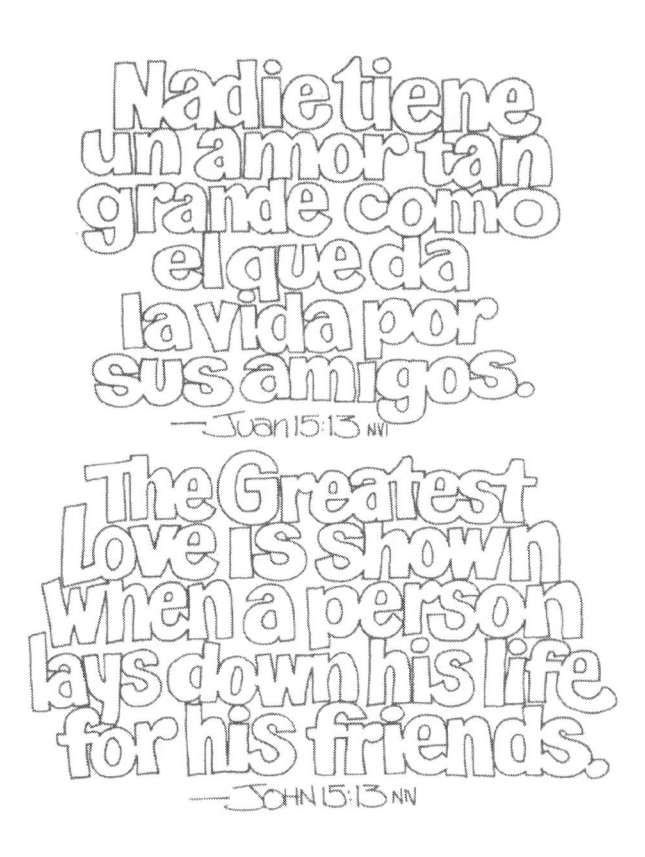

Nadie tiene un amor tan grande como el que da la vida por sus amigos.
—Juan 15:13 NVI

The Greatest Love is Shown when a person lays down his life for his friends.
—John 15:13 NIV

24

Neil

I'll stay for ten minutes.

November 10, 1984

"Joy, now remember. You promised me. Ten minutes, max," Neil pleaded.

Joy turned her Mercedes onto Turkey Creek Road. "I remember. Just ten minutes."She pulled into the grassy parking area at STAR. "Thanks, Neil, thanks for doing this—for coming to see what my friends do here."

Neil Ruda ducked his head to enter the office-trailer. We greeted Joy and Neil warmly—any friend of Joy and Jack Eachon's was a friend of ours.

Joe walked with Neil into the studio, the control room, the prop storage area, the duplication area. As Joe explained our vision for using television and radio to reach children and adults, Neil's heart began to soften.

"What do you do, Neil? What is your area of expertise?" Joe asked, with an obvious ulterior motive.

"I'm coming from Teen Challenge where I've been working for about three years ... I love computers—"

Joe jumped at the word! "Computers!? Exactly what we need. Would you stay? Help us?"

"Give me a few minutes," Neil mumbled. He walked outside, stood under the old, oak tree by the front door, and then he ambled down the grassy slope toward the woods. Looking heavenward, he said, "God, is this where You want me? Now? Should I stay here for a few days? Help these people?"

Sighing, Neil headed back to the office. "Joy, why don't you go on back home? I'll stay for a while."

He did. For five years.

That first afternoon, Neil asked what he could do. Joe said, "Well, this hallway sure needs vacuuming." So Neil vacuumed. Then Joe called, "Neil, could you come run Camera 2? It's the wide shot, and is usually just a static shot." So Neil ran camera. The next morning, Neil showed up with the courage to ask about his salary. "Uh, actually," Joe informed him, "there is no salary. You will be a *MAPS* missionary (Missionary And Placement Service) which means you need to raise your own support through family and friends." Neil almost fainted! Then he started calling friends and writing letters to raise his monthly support.

Neil brought us into the computer age. As he learned more and more, he taught us—the little bit we could comprehend.

We had accumulated hundreds of hours of "raw footage." Whenever we did an outside shoot, we deliberately also shot such things as clouds, children playing, old folks talking—anything we could ever possibly want to use as "B-roll," a video insert to enhance a show. Neil computerized our Raw Footage Library, indicating what, when, where in the world, and where on the tape. Example: Market place, vegetables, Mexico 1980, Tape 6, @ 23:10–23:30.

One day, Neil turned his hand to puppeteering in the *Secret Place* backyard gang. However, that career was short-lived (like my puppeteering stint); we both used our talents better in other areas.

Others were also joining our STAR team: Harold and Bea Mintle joined us for marketing and distribution. Gerald and Gerri Jackson arrived to be in charge of new construction. We needed to increase publicity, so Neil prepared brochures. He designed order blanks, catalogues, graphs, distribution charts, and newsletters; he wrote answers to viewers' write-in letters; he prepared reports and booklets for our annual "Jubilee" open-house fund-raiser. For our mission's head-quarters, he prepared distinguished-looking, bound folders with reports to show productions and distribution, complete with bar graphs, pie charts, and maps.

One of the formats Neil designed for *Lugar Secreto*

***

George Davis, a missionary pilot, came to STAR to shoot educational programs for International Correspondence Institute (ICI, now Global University). George did not present the lessons himself; he brought "talent" to teach these lessons and other courses as well. Wonderful people, including Lucas Muñoz, Ilidio da Silva, Jerónimo Pérez, Carlos Jiménez, Bill and Hope Brooke, Floyd Woodworth, Sam Balius, David Godwin, and John Bueno.

Evelyn produced the shows, and George ran the teleprompter. In those days, teleprompters were not yet digitized, and it took hours to set up everything. The two main components consisted of a motorized conveyer belt and a monitor-mirror apparatus attached to the camera tripod.

First, Neil typed into his computer the script from the "teacher" (in Spanish, of course, a real challenge!) and carefully set the narrow margins. Then, he printed the script out on continuous-feed paper. He took the very long paper (containing twenty minutes' worth of talking) to the studio and stretched the first part of the script onto the eight-foot conveyor belt. The belt fed the script to the far end underneath a small black-and-white camera mounted up about two feet. From the camera, cables ran to two monitors (small black-and-white TVs). One monitor was for George, the other hung on the tripod of Camera 2 in the middle of the studio floor. That monitor was mounted in front of the camera, below the lens, facing up. Above the monitor was a slanted mirror that reflected the script onto a clear, glass pane in front of the camera lens. A large, black cloth hood covered the whole apparatus, because extraneous light nullified the reflection.

The *talent* (presenter-teacher) would walk onto the set, greet the viewer, and begin to read the teleprompter-glass pane as the script moved slowly up the screen. The teacher appeared to look directly at the viewer.

But how did the script move, at just the correct speed, not too fast and not too slowly? From the conveyor belt ran a cable with a remote control device attached to the end. The device was sort of like a hotdog bun. George held the device in his left hand, and swiveled the "bun" around and around with his right hand. The faster he turned, the faster the belt ran, and the faster the words flew up the monitor screen. There was quite a bit of "play" in the remote control, so to start without "running away" was a challenge! And timing the continuous speed to the pace of the speaker was an art! One day, perspiring heavily, George muttered, "Flying an airplane is *easy* compared to this!"

***

Lucas Muñoz shared George's terror of teleprompters. Dear, sweet Hermano Lucas, from Peru, had never been on television before. He was dark-complexioned, short, rotund, and in his 60s, I guess. As floor director, I sat down with him and went over the list of do's and don'ts: do walk confidently onto the set (when I cue you), do stop at the strip of tape on the floor, then, do turn to the camera and look straight into the lens. Don't "eyeball" by looking from side to side. Greet the viewer. Singular. We know many students will watch the video, but one set of ears is listening to you, and we want you to speak directly to him or to her.

Hermano Lucas nodded. He stood just off set awaiting my cue. We rolled tape. I motioned to him to walk onto the set. He hesitated, took a deep breath, and then walked on, and on, and kept on walking, past his tape on the floor. Sweat beaded his make-up. Cut! Let's try that again, and this time, don't be nervous. Just walk here, to this strip of tape.

Take two. He walked to the tape, stopped, and froze. Take three. Take four. Each time, Evelyn and I comforted him, handed him paper towels to mop the sweat off his face (forget trying to re-apply make-up), and reassured him that he would do great this time ... as we tried take after take after take. Finally we finished one lesson. That evening we showed him what we had shot. He looked great! His confidence budded and blossomed before our eyes. The next day he did much better, and the following day even better. By the time the series concluded, and we re-shot Lesson 1, he looked like the professional he had become.

***

Carlos Jiménez was another story! Carlos, a Colombian, was confident on set, and did a great job. But the first morning he came to the studio dressed in stripes and red plaids—a horrible combination for television. We couldn't believe it—Evelyn had sent him the suggestions for clothing. And, in fact, Joe had talked with him—long distance to Colombia—about bringing TV-appropriate clothes. It was time to roll tape, and Joe didn't want to hurt Carlos' feelings, but there was no way we could shoot with him looking like that! He seemed oblivious to Joe's hints, wanting to get on with the program. But finally, Carlos began to laugh—he had deliberately worn the wrong clothes in order to tease Joe!

We finished the series with Carlos and as the last shots ended, Joe said in my earpiece, "Tell Carlos we have to shoot that last segment over again. My fault." So, as floor director, I relayed the message. We backed up the conveyor belt, found the spot on the script and began to shoot. About two minutes in, Joe said in our headsets, "OK everyone. This is a joke. The original footage was fine. Everyone, tighten down your cameras and just walk quietly out of the studio. George, just lay down the teleprompter control and walk quietly away. Camera 1, walk away. Camera 3, Camera 2, walk away. Margaret, follow them." We walked quietly away and left Carlos alone in the studio talking his head off, trying to improvise until the script moved on again.

We gathered in the control room to watch. Finally, Carlos realized we were pulling a trick *on him* and he burst out laughing!

But what a marvelous machine that teleprompter was! Emily Bressette and the Missionette girls from Ohio had bought it for us. I loved speaking at their retreat and at similar ones for girls and ladies in Florida, West Virginia, and Virginia.

In another area of expertise, Neil set up a new, computerized bookkeeping program and helped Evelyn to become proficient on the computer.

Every year we held an open house fund-raiser. We would work really hard to clean up everything inside and outside the facility. One day, Evelyn and Joe were raking leaves in front of the building when, suddenly, a car drove up. As an elderly man got out and approached them. Joe murmured to Evelyn, "He looks familiar—but I can't think of his name."

Evelyn whispered back, "I know his face; I know he's from Lake Worth—he is a large donor, on my computer list. You keep him talking; I'll go look him up. And I'll send Roland outside. He is good at names."

Evelyn hurried inside, and sent Roland out on the porch while Joe and the man conversed. Finally Evelyn came back, stood beside Roland, and greeted Al Garrison by name. Mr. Garrison then handed her a nice check for STAR and turned to Roland, saying, "Greet your wife for me."

Roland grinned, "I will ... actually, here she is." Evelyn then stammered, "And you give your wife our love."

"I will ... when I get to heaven. She died last year." With that, Al smiled, got in his car, and drove away. Joe and Evelyn and Roland doubled over in laughter. And, fortunately, "Al" continued to donate to STAR.

***

Evidence of Neil Ruda's skills was reflected in a letter from Monroe Grams, *The Christian Training Network*, written April 15, 1987, after a shoot we had just done for CTN.

> "I came away from that pleasant and idyllic setting with a sense of real satisfaction last Thursday ... I must express to you all how great it was to work together. We had a job to do, we were convinced that it was of vital importance for Latin America, and everyone cooperated so beautifully until the last lesson was finished ... and even to the retaping of #1. Thanks a million for everything. You made us feel at home. We sensed an atmosphere of love and appreciation. You guys are involved in one of the greatest ministries open to the church today ... We salute you for having the vision, for keeping your noses to the grindstone even when the going is rough, and for producing an end product that is 'second to none.' In going over the rough footage, I am thoroughly pleased with what we have. It communicates. It's close and quite warm. And the content is of vital importance ... Again, our heartfelt gratitude."

Every year, Neil's reports grew to reveal expanded ministry: In 1985 we distributed 8,087 video programs and 4,396 audio programs. In 1986 we distributed over 18,000 video and audio programs. Some programs were broadcast on local and international stations. Others on videocassettes were used in Bible clubs, schools, churches, orphanages, and home groups.

Countries included:

Argentina	Australia
Bahamas	Austria
Belize	Belgium
Bolivia	Britain
Brazil	Cameroon
Canary Islands	Denmark
Chile	Equatorial Guinea
Colombia	Germany
Costa Rica	Ghana
Cuba	India
Dominican Republic	Ireland
Ecuador	Israel
El Salvador	Kenya
Guatemala	Nigeria
Guyana	Philippines
Haiti	Scotland
Honduras	Sierra Leone
Jamaica	Singapore
Mexico	Spain
Netherland Antilles	Switzerland
Nicaragua	Thailand
Panama	Uganda
Paraguay	Venezuela
Peru	and throughout the
Puerto Rico	United States
Uruguay	(including Alaska)

Neil on camera

Carol Young and Neil working on a fun project

***

After five fruitful years with STAR, Neil moved to our mission headquarters, where his missionary career continues—using his computer skills—even as I write these words!

A Place for People, Puppets, and Cockroach Soup

"HOW CAN I HELP MY HUNGRY NEIGHBOR?"
"¿COMO PUEDO AYUDAR A MI VECINO HAMBRIENTO?"

25

Judy

We will tell the next generation.
Psalm 78:4

What a debt of gratitude STAR owes to Judy Bartel Graner! She first came to us from Colombia in 1980. As I've mentioned earlier, Judy brought with her Maritza and Sara Segura, who have been indispensable as writers, puppeteers and dear friends. Judy also introduced us to a young missionary by the name of Steve Graner, who just happened to be available in 1984 to help us shoot *Lugar Secreto*. Before the next scheduled shoot, Steve and Judy were married. They moved to Santa Marta, Colombia, so that Steve could continue to reach into the jungle to his beloved Wayúu.

Judy and Steve Graner with friends

Judy loves to teach. She taught many of our educational programs for adults, and as the puppet *profesora*, Doña Isabelita, Judy presided over a classroom of unruly puppet students. And her Don Manolo character with his sloooooow Spanish drawl counsels puppet after puppet from his kiosk on the *Lugar Secreto* plaza. (See page 164.) Puppeteering is demeaning and demanding, but Judy never complained, even when her arms ached and her back would spasm with pain.

I mentioned previously that Judy talked for years about developing a bilingual coloring book (Spanish/English) as a giveaway to the thousands of children who wrote to Bobo after watching a show on TV. She eventually accomplished this goal—as you can see—because we have replicated throughout this book some of her excellent drawings from that coloring book.

As storyteller on *Lugar Secreto*, Judy is always "live" while puppets Tomasito and Rosita accompany her. Being "live on camera" means that people recognize Judy as she travels—and travel she does! Having now obtained her doctoral degree in Intercultural Studies, she flies frequently into almost every Latin American country where she teaches in Bible colleges and in post-graduate seminars for Latin American Advanced School of Theology *(LAAST)* and *Instituto de Superación Ministerial* (*ISUM*).

As Judy sat at a restaurant in Costa Rica, a waitress stared at her from the side of the room. The waitress nudged her supervisor, whispered, and gestured toward Judy. Suddenly the waitress hurried across the room and blurted, "Are you Judy? Can you really be *the Judy* who saved my life?" Tears formed and rolled from her eyes as the waitress realized she really was face-to-face with Judy.

The waitress stuttered, "Last year my husband left me. Walked out and left me alone with my two young daughters. I had no income. No help. No hope. I decided to end my life. But on that particular afternoon, the girls begged me to watch television with them. So I sat on the couch in front of the TV, one girl on each side. I knew that soon they would have no mother. I placed my arms around my daughters for the last time. I glanced up at the screen to see what intrigued my girls so much. And there you were, Judy, looking straight at me. Telling me that God loved me. Loved *me*. I decided to live one more day. To watch you one more time.

A Place for People, Puppets, and Cockroach Soup

"The following day I saw the entire program. I smiled as my daughters laughed at the puppets. Then, once again, Judy, you talked to me. For two weeks I watched as my heart softened toward God and my faith grew to know that God indeed loved me. I prayed with you. You advised me to look for a church to attend. I did, and today I am alive—because of you. Thank you, Judy, for saving my life."

One day Judy received an email from Ramón, a man from Cerrejón, Albania Guajira, Colombia. Ramón said he thought Judy and Steve were wasting their time participating in *Lugar Secreto* kid stuff. That is, until he had a son and bought some videos for him. Ramón wrote, "Now, years later, God has taught me to 'shut my mouth' because I see the EXCELLENT work that you all have done for families. My little son has given his heart to '*Critina*' and Judy. Thank you for helping form his character."

On one of her trips to Costa Rica, Judy was standing in line at the airport to go through customs when people recognized her and called across the terminal "*¡Es Judy del Lugar Secreto!*" So, she was prepared to be recognized by the time she arrived at the Bible College for her month-long seminar. But she was not prepared for a woman's screams in the cafeteria.

Judy stood in line with the other professors and students to pick up her chicken and rice and fried plantains. All of a sudden, from across the counter, a woman who was volunteering to help for this special seminar spotted Judy. "Judy!" she screamed. "Is that really you? Judy?!" The woman rushed around the counter and grabbed Judy's arm. "Oh, you must come to my house! You must! Please! My son, Oscar, he must meet you. He will not believe this!"

The woman would not explain any further, but insisted that Judy come to her house. They made the arrangements, and a few hours later, Judy sat drinking tea on a strange couch in a stranger's house. The woman kept looking at a clock on the side table. "Almost time," she murmured, her eyes dancing with excitement. She cocked her head as she heard a key being inserted in the door. She held her breath as the knob turned and the door began to open.

A college kid stuck his head through the doorway. He glanced at his mother. Then stared at Judy. He gasped. His head tilted forward. His eyes bulged. He dropped his books on the floor. His keys skittered across the tile.

He ran forward, arms outstretched. Tears glistened on his cheeks, as he cried, "*Mamá, Mamá, ¡Mamá Judy!*" He hugged Judy, rocking her back and forth as he repeated over and over, "You are my mother, my spiritual mother. *Mi mamá, mi Judy.*"

And then, Oscar sat on the floor in front of the couch. He smiled at Judy, held her hand, and began his story:

Mamá Judy, when I was nine years old, my dad bought a television set. It was so special that he put the TV in his office, here at home, and placed the remote control on a high shelf. Dad ordered me and my twin sisters never to touch the remote control because he was the only person who knew how to operate it.

Well, of course, the next day when I came home from school for lunch, I wanted to watch TV. But, Dad wanted to take his siesta. So while he was sleeping … I sneaked into the office. I climbed up, grabbed the remote control, and pushed the red button. Onto the screen popped—you! I could not take my eyes off the screen. You, *Mamá Judy*, began to tell me a story. You looked straight into my eyes. I felt your love, you spoke to *me*. I listened carefully to every word you said. You held your blue Bible, and you told me it is the Word of God himself. I prayed with you. Then some puppets talked and sang. As soon as the program ended, I turned off the TV, replaced the remote, and sneaked up to my bed to finish my siesta.

Every day for ten years I watched you on *Lugar Secreto*. I became friends with Bobo and Cristina and Tomasito and Rosita and Gonzalo el Malo and el Capitán and the Professor and Carlos and Don Manolo. I know every song, every Bible verse, every story. I prayed with you to receive Jesus as my Savior. You not only led me to faith in Christ, but I realize now that you also discipled me through systematic Bible teaching.

And the dramas! I laughed as those puppets acted out everyday life situations, but they were helping me learn to apply the biblical principles to my daily life. And I loved the music!

For ten years you lived, secretly, in my heart as my family. But I could never tell my parents. They despised evangelicals and would not understand my new faith. They would have forbidden me ever to watch the program again. (Oscar's mother nodded her head.)

Then, *Mamá Judy,* (Oscar grinned and looked at his mother from the corner of his eye) four years ago, when I was nineteen years old, Mother came to me and said quietly, "Sunday we are going to church. Do not tell your father." I told her that we always go to Mass on Sundays. She said that this would be different; we would attend the Assemblies of God church. I knew that Mother walked every morning for exercise. I did not know that she had begun walking with Sharon Marlin, a missionary. And that Sharon had invited Mother in for tea. And that Sharon had led Mother to faith in Jesus Christ.

I answered, "All right. I'll go to church with you." I did *not* tell her anything more.

Sunday morning, my mother, twin sisters, and I dressed as usual "for church." We left the house and headed for the Protestant church. We were all scared. We had no idea what awaited us, once inside a forbidden building.

A man greeted us at the gate. He led us into the building, showed us where we could sit. No saints adorned the walls. No candles burned. No one wore long robes. No one burned incense.

Then a young man stood up front, strummed his guitar and began to sing. I knew this song! We sang it on *Lugar Secreto*! I sang along, my voice soft at first but swelling to show that I knew every word. Mother nudged me in the ribs with her elbow, "How do you know this song?" I smiled and kept singing. We sang another song. I knew it, too!

A few minutes later, a man took a black book and said he would read from the Bible. Uh-oh. Big Trouble. My heart pounded. That is *not* the Bible. Not the *real* Bible. This book is *black*. The real Bible is *blue*. I know because every day my Judy holds up the big, blue Bible, she points to it and says, "This is God's Word. If something is in this book, believe it. If not, do not believe it."

The man began to read. I knew these words! They were words that Judy read to me! Then the man asked for anyone who wanted to publicly acknowledge Jesus as Lord and Savior to come forward. Mother and I stepped out into the aisle and walked to the front.

I whispered to Mother that I must speak to this man, privately, as soon as possible. There was something I *must* clear up.

When the prayers concluded, I motioned that I needed to talk to the man. Pastor, they called him. "Pastor," I explained, my forehead creased with concern, "Why do you have the wrong Bible? The real Bible is not black, it is blue. I watch *Lugar Secreto* and listen to Judy every day. She always says her blue Bible is the Word of God."

The pastor's eyes filled with tears. He understood my confusion. "Son, the Bible can have a cover of any color. My cover happens to be black, but the inside is the same—look, here are the words Judy reads to you—from her Bible with the cover in blue."

Oscar, still holding Judy's hand, looked deeply into her eyes. "And so, *Mamá Judy,* I am 23 years of age now, and I am studying to be a chiropractor. Both of my sisters have accepted Jesus, and for four years, we have been attending the church. My sisters sing in the worship team and work with the other teenagers at the church. Thank you for being *mi mamá espiritual.* I love you so much!"

Judy looked at Oscar, at his face unknown to her until just a few minutes ago. Her heart filled with love as she held his hand and gazed at "her son," and she realized—with the certainty that only God can give—that she has many sons and daughters just waiting to meet her in heaven someday: her other "children" who are coming to know Jesus through the foolishness of a puppet show.

***

During the writing of this book, Judy's beloved husband, Steve, went home to heaven. However, his legacy continues through videos and through the lives he touched in Colombia and around the world. Throughout his many years as a missionary, Steve prayed a prayer similar to this with hundreds of adults and children:

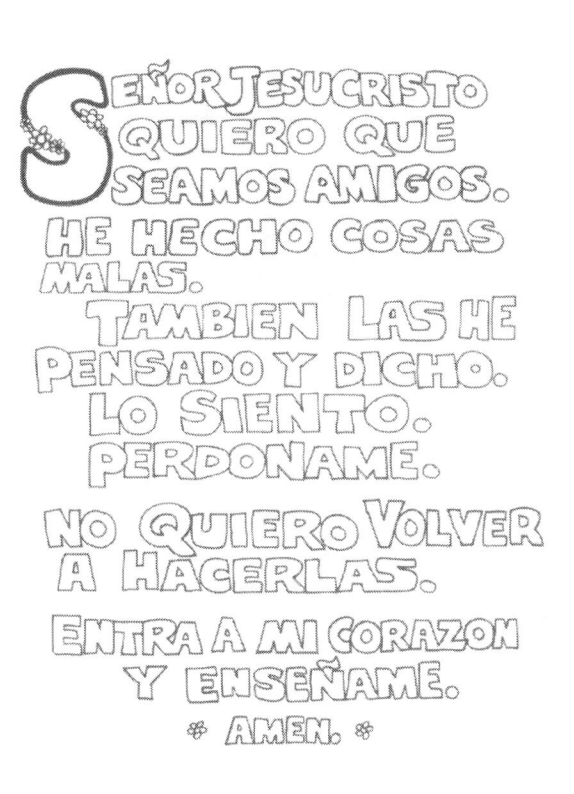

> SEÑOR JESUCRISTO QUIERO QUE SEAMOS AMIGOS.
> HE HECHO COSAS MALAS.
> TAMBIEN LAS HE PENSADO Y DICHO.
> LO SIENTO.
> PERDONAME.
> NO QUIERO VOLVER A HACERLAS.
> ENTRA A MI CORAZON Y ENSEÑAME.
> ❀ AMEN. ❀

ESTA ORACION TE AYUDARA A SER HIJO DE DIOS...

Lord Jesus, I want to be your friend. I've done things that are bad. I've thought and said things that are bad. I'm sorry. Forgive me. I don't want to do them anymore. Please come into my heart and teach me. Amen.

BAD WILL TURN GOOD IF WE CONFESS OUR SINS TO JESUS.
EL MAL SE TORNARA EN BIEN SI CONFESAMOS NUESTROS PECADOS A JESUCRISTO.

26

Ana

Guatemala, November 1987

Joe's heart lurched. Sweat beaded his brow. He would be trampled! Just in front of him the wire, double gate of the stadium bowed toward him. Thousands of children pushed and chanted, "Bo-bo, Bo-bo." How could Joe escape from being crushed by the crowd? To his right he saw a small opening under the lip of the concrete bleachers. He scurried into it. Just in time. The gates opened. The crowd surged into the stadium.

A few months earlier, in Florida, the phone on my desk rang. I answered, "Hello, *STAR Ministries*. This is Margaret."

"*Habla Ana Agüero de Guatemala.* (This is Ana Aguero from Guatemala.) Your program *Lugar Secreto* is on television here every day. The children love it. We want you to come to Guatemala for a children's rally."

I was shocked and surprised. "Ana, thank you so much for the invitation, but it would be very expensive to travel so far with a television team. Thank you, though, for the invitation."

"Margarita, I will call you again. Be praying about this!"

Several weeks later, my phone rang again.

Ana said, "I'm calling to tell you that I am still looking for a site for a children's rally. I'm the secretary who answers all the write-ins to *Lugar Secreto* here in Guatemala City, and I know we would have at least 100 children, maybe even 200, who would attend a rally. Please say you'll come to Guatemala."

Ana talked on and on, until finally, I said, "All right, all right. Let me talk to the team here, and we'll call our mission leaders in Missouri to see if they'll give us permission."

They did. So, we began to plan the program. Sarita and Maritza wrote the script. We made a list of props and costumes and sound effects that we would need.

Ana called again, "I've been thinking that a church is too small a venue for the rally. So I'm considering renting a larger place. I'll let you know what I find."

A few days later, Ana called back, "I've found it! I've already made a deposit … on a larger place."

"You have? Larger?"

"Yes, a basketball stadium."

"What!? Ana! A stadium?"

"Yes, I've already put down a deposit."

"Ana!"

"The stadium seats 6,000 people."

"Ana!"

"Many children will come, you'll see. We will print announcements in the newspapers. We will hand out invitations in the schools. We need you to make some 'spots' with Bobo and Toni for advertisement on radio and television."

I could not believe it! A 6,000 seat stadium? *Maybe* 200 children *might* come … but they would just rattle around in that large stadium. I thought, "We're going to be so embarrassed."

Then Ana added, "Oh, by the way, could some of us come to the airport to greet you? To welcome you to the country?" I assured her that would be fine.

We filmed a "commercial" with Toni and Bobo. Bobo is packing his suitcase while Toni watches. Bobo says, "Toni, you are too young to go to Guatemala. I'm going to the basketball stadium, but you can't come. You're too little." Bobo turns his back to find something else to put in his suitcase. While his back is turned, Toni hops inside the suitcase and scrunches down underneath Bobo's junk. Toni turns to the camera, pacifier waving, and whispers, "Don't tell Bobo, but I'll see you in Guatemala!"

As we finalized our plans, twenty people signed up to make the trip. Even our mentor and first pastor, Tom Waldron with his wife,

A Place for People, Puppets, and Cockroach Soup

Maxine, wanted to go. We booked the tickets for the cast and crew, which included: Cristina, Judy, Maritza, Sarita, Carlos, Amanda, Alan, Paula, Nelsa, Carol, Gerald, Gerri, and John.

Finally, the day arrived, and our airplane approached the airfield in Guatemala City. Some passengers stared out the windows and exclaimed, "Look down there at that huge crowd! All those people in front of the airport! Some big celebrity must be arriving today."

We deplaned, walked across the tarmac, and entered the large terminal where we would go through customs. We stood in a queue with our passports in hand, our carry-on luggage at our side. The line inched forward while government officials scurried around looking bewildered. They walked the line, searching every face. "*No. Este no. No. No es él. No.*" (No, not him. He's not the one.)

They scrutinized the entire line of passengers. The airline and government officials shook their heads. They marched to the airplane. Boarded it. Came back out, down the stairs to the tarmac. They looked over the luggage being unloaded.

Befuddled, they reentered the terminal and stood in a group to one side. They seemed anxious. Panicky, almost. Then, suddenly, I could overhear them talking. "*No vino. Bobo no vino.*" (He didn't come. Bobo didn't come.)

Without even thinking, I walked quickly toward them. "Excuse me. I heard you say '*Bobo no vino.*' Are you talking about the puppet Bobo?"

"Yes!" they sighed. "He was supposed to be on this flight! But he didn't come."

"Yes—he did! He is over there. In the blue bag that my husband, Joe, is holding."

Relief flooded their faces as they rushed to Joe's side. "Hurry! Take Bobo out and put him on. There are thousands of children waiting to welcome him!"

Then it dawned on us what the sound was that we could hear coming from the lobby area. People were chanting loudly. "Bo-bo. Bo-bo. Bo-bo."

"Hurry. Put Bobo on. There are 2,000 children on the balcony. We've had to use crowd control techniques to keep them from falling off. Your plane was three hours late. Hurry, put Bobo on. They are waiting to greet Bobo!"

But Bobo is not a suit puppet. A person does not "put him on." He is a large, hand-held puppet. Joe places his right arm in Bobo's head, his left arm in Bobo's left arm and hand. A second person operates the right arm. Plus, we didn't even have Bobo's legs with us in the blue carry-on bag.

I could just picture us walking out into that lobby area, Bobo dangling on Joe's arms. No feet, only a half-body. The children would be *so* disappointed! To them, Bobo was real. He rode a bike, he swung from a rope Tarzan-style, he talked on the phone. He ate roaches, and cooked delicious roach soup.

My heart sank. How could we disappoint these children? And yet, how could we not?

"Oh, God," I prayed a quick, panic-stricken prayer. "What can we do?"

Suddenly, God gave us an idea. The government officials could gather around Joe, surrounding him so that no one would notice his arms lifted up. He could hold Bobo up on their shoulders. The men, in suit and tie, would be Bobo's bodyguards!

By this time, Ana had managed to talk her way through the cloud of government officials to arrive at our side. She was a tiny twenty-year-old with beautiful dimples in both cheeks. With her was gray-haired Walter Haydus, a veteran missionary who could have retired years earlier. But he was the sponsor of *Lugar Secreto* in Guatemala. He was the one who had hired Ana to be his secretary in charge of children's ministries! Now, Walter and Ana proudly joined "the bodyguards."

And so, Bobo marched out into that lobby with his entourage surrounding him. He was "real"! He waved to the crowd gathered on the balcony. They chanted and cheered and clapped and stomped and waved back.

"Keep walking," said one "bodyguard." They walked out the front door of the airport, across the street and into a large amphitheatre where 3,000 more children were waiting! They, too, were chanting and clapping.

The atmosphere sizzled with joy. Thousands of smiling faces beamed at Bobo and Cristina and Captain Alan. The children surrounded us in the amphitheatre. They clapped and shouted even louder, "Bo-bo!"

Ana and her team had written a song to welcome Bobo to Guatemala. All the children sang it, very loudly. They'd had time to practice and memorize it because our plane arrived so late.

Ana had recruited a dozen helpers who dressed as clowns. They had sung, told stories, passed out balloons, and somehow entertained 3,000 children for the three hours they had been waiting!

The Guatemalan newspaper covered Bobo's arrival at the airport!

Ana had prepared a puppet stage, so Bobo and Cristina and Alan made a brief presentation and then, of course, we invited all the children to come to the basketball stadium on Friday for the rally.

Back in the airport, the government officials wanted Bobo's autograph. (Bobo always signs his name with the B drawn backwards.) Bobo talked to everyone and signed paper after paper.

Finally, one government official noticed Joe standing behind Bobo. "Sir, do you speak Spanish?" We laughed and laughed because Bobo was so real that the man couldn't believe Joe "operated" Bobo!

Bobo rushing through the airport with his bodyguards
on the way to the amphitheatre

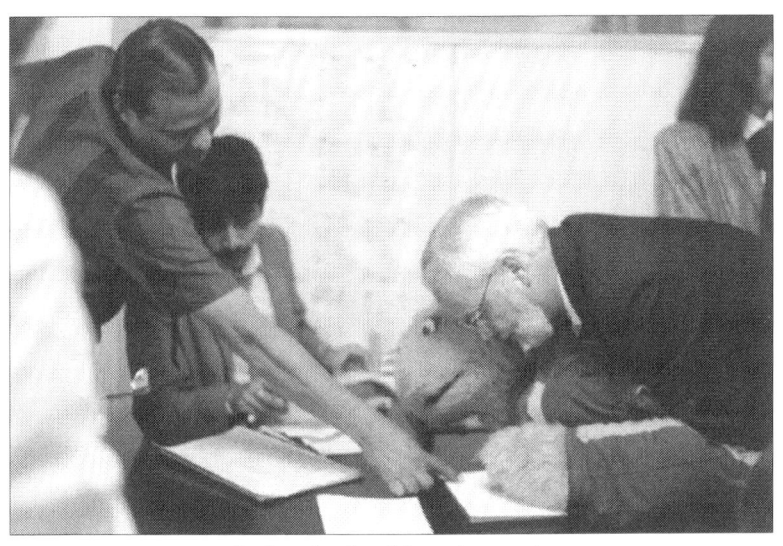

Bobo signing his autograph
for government and airline officials

Ana had a bus waiting to take us to our quaint hotel. Three stories, small elevator, cozy dining room. We loved it! The staff waited on our every need for the five days we were there. Breakfast was ready before we could even ask for it, and Joe especially enjoyed the oatmeal (which he usually hates). The cook placed sugar in a large pot (to brown the sugar), then added milk, then added the old fashioned oats. She simmered the oats until they were tender, but made sure there was more brown-sugar-milk than oatmeal. Delicious.

All that week we rehearsed, built sets, and prepared the basketball stadium for Friday's rally. Ana whisked Crysti and Joe away to television stations, for interviews with Bobo and Toni.

The excitement was contagious, and Friday morning we could hardly wait to go to the stadium. We arrived early to find the stadium—filled! At least 6,000 children were crammed onto the concrete bleachers. Ana's helpers scurried around: ladies distributing questionnaires; girls (*Misioneritas* in their blue skirts and white blouses) handing out gospel tracts; and boys (*Exploradores* in their dark blue trousers and white shirts with ties) serving as ushers. The atmosphere quivered with happy bedlam! The helpers soon ran out of materials, because even Ana had not anticipated such a large crowd.

We had barely begun the show, when Ana came to us backstage. She wrung her hands in anguish. "There are still more children out in the road. What can we do? Can we do another show?" We replied that of course we would!

Waiting in line to see Bobo

The first show ended, the children and parents exited to our right. The stadium emptied. That's when Joe decided to make a trip to the rest room, to our left, and that's when he ran into the stadium gates—with almost disastrous results. The gates bowed toward him with thousands of kids pushing to enter. He scooted under the lip of the bleachers just in time.

Whoosh, those children and their parents flooded into the stadium. And the stadium filled for the second time—6,000 more kids!

A short time later, from behind the set, Joe heard a man's voice booming out from the crowd shouting something about "Bobo." Joe's face paled. A heckler, no doubt! Trouble! Someone here to ridicule a Christian show for children. The deep voice shouted louder, "Bo-bo! Bo-bo!" Joe stiffened. Then the children chimed in, shouting even louder, "Bo-bo! Bo-bo!" Suddenly Joe realized that the man wasn't heckling! He was chanting for the show to begin! The children's voices surrounded his. The swell grew louder and louder, resonating from wall to wall.

Tears rolled down Joe's cheeks. His heart melted. Sobs shook his body. He clearly remembered having stated, earlier, "It's all right that no one knows me. If we can reach children, and adults, through this 'silly' puppet show, through me being *Bobo*, then I yield to whatever God wants, however He wants to do this." And God had used him. Used him to touch thousands of people. No one chanted "Joe." But, "Bo-bo," beloved puppet, blessed by God. Creative innovation anointed for a new generation.

The lights came up. Judy and Alan, Carlos and Cristina greeted the children. Bobo popped up and talked to the children. Puppets Tomasito and Rosita talked with Bobo. And then, Toni peeked out of the suitcase and the kids screamed with delight.

Before we were very far into the second program, Ana came to us. Again. More children in the road. All the way down to the highway. Could we stay for a third show? Yes, of course.

As soon as the second show ended, Ana handed us fast-food chicken dinners. We would need to eat quickly, the stadium was filling up. For the third time.

By now, several of us needed to use the rest room. Judy and I, along with Maxine Waldron, pushed our way through the crowd. As we approached the rest room doors, we could smell the pungent odor. We looked down and saw overflowing toilet water seeping toward us. Items, unmentionable, floated in the water. Maxine gagged, turned around and said, "I think I can wait!" Judy and I could not wait. Gingerly we stepped through the "water." There were no stalls, no privacy, no paper. Obviously, the stadium management had not anticipated so many people, either.

Slowly, we pushed back through the crowd to the stage.

We could not believe our eyes. The stadium had filled for the third time—a total of 18,000 children!

All of our team members were profoundly moved. Never in our wildest imaginations could we envision touching so many children, in person, at one time.

After each show, we hugged as many children as possible. We touched their hands, we patted their shoulders. Our tears splattered on top of their heads. We kissed cheeks of faces we had only imagined and prayed for. We had sent videotapes for years to country after country. Missionaries had told us of good results in one country after another. But this was the first time for us to see for ourselves the results of our programs.

A glimpse inside the stadium

We had kept "our nose to the grindstone" trying to produce as much software as possible. Now, we realized that all those lonely hours were worth it! Now, the pain morphed into profound joy. Now, we literally touched children who "knew" us. Whose lives had been changed because of our vision and hard work. It seemed like a dream. The sounds and smells and moving masses of people. It was unreal. Incomprehensible. Exhilarating and exhausting.

When the shows finally ended, after we had been nine hours on our feet, we collapsed onto the seats of the bus. Paula squealed, "Hurry back to the hotel! I have to go to the rest room! Bad!" Everyone joined in the cry. We laughed the free laughter of those overcome with weariness and with the certainty of a job well done.

Ana's idea, her vision of "what-could-happen," continues to amaze me and it continues to impact thousands of Guatemalan and American lives.

Several years later, Ana married Rick Salvato, a medical missionary, and they moved to the States. She and her husband and four children continue to minister with medical teams.

Ana and her family (see her dimples?)
(photo courtesy of *Pentecostal Evangel*)

"Jesus is MY Captain"
Cristo es MI capitán.

27

Frieda

December 24, 1916—March 5, 1992

Frieda Arnold, my mother, loved to come and help us during the month-long *Lugar Secreto* productions. Sometimes she would stay at our house and have a meal on the table when we walked in from the studio. But she especially liked for us to park our camper-trailer beside the STAR buildings, so that she could stay there and be available to baby-sit Jennifer and Kyndal—Crysti and Doug's babies, Mom's great-grandbabies.

Frieda Arnold

After Daddy retired as pastor of Brownsville Assembly and subsequently passed away in 1981, Mom sold their house and moved into an apartment complex in Pensacola. But, her health gradually deteriorated due to diabetes and congestive heart failure, and, frequently, she would be hospitalized. Then she would recover and go back to her apartment. She couldn't drive anymore, so the church van picked her up every Sunday morning.

As Joe and I were walking into our house, about noon on Sunday, February 16, 1992, the phone was ringing. It was my sister Jan. "Mom is in the hospital again and it doesn't look good. The doctor says she probably won't make it this time. You'd better come as quickly as you can." Mom had not felt like going to church that morning, so she stayed home, and began to feel increasingly ill. She dialed 911 and went by ambulance to Sacred Heart Hospital. A nurse called Brownsville Assembly to contact Jan and my brother-in-law, Barry, during the church service. Jan played the organ for the church and Barry served as an usher.

By the time Joe and I arrived at the hospital, Mom was in ICU. Jan and Barry, with their daughter, Kim, and son, Shawn, were already there. We gathered in a semi-circle around Mom's bed. She was pale, her eyes were closed, and she was hooked up to various machines. We reminisced for a while, and then Jan said, "Mom, if you see Daddy before we do, tell him we love him and miss him."

Mom nodded her head and said haltingly, "If ... I ... see ... Dad ... before ... you ... do ... I'll tell him ... I doubt if a one of you makes it to heaven."

Stunned into silence, we gasped for a breath, and then, simultaneously, burst out laughing! Our Mom is lying there dying—and she is making jokes!

The next day, when Joe and I walked into her room, he approached her bed and said, "Gram, this is your good-lookin' son-in-law." Mom replied, "Hello, Barry."

That first day, Jan and I stayed very late with Mom. Finally, Jan told me to go on to Mom's apartment and get some rest. Jan would stay all night at the hospital.

When I walked into the apartment about midnight, Joe said, "Don't sit down. The neighbor lady, Marietta, is waiting up for you. She saw the ambulance take Mom away and she is really worried. I promised her you'd give her a report."

I stepped next door, knocked softly, and an elderly lady opened the door. Marietta was in her late 80s, her body frail, her hands knotted with arthritis. Her apartment's thermostat was set to "hot"! She invited me in, and I sat on the couch. She sat beside me. I reached out and took her hand.

Marietta fretted, "Is Frieda all right? Will she be home soon? I am so worried about her."

"Marietta, Mom is very ill. I'm afraid she is not going to make it this time."

Marietta's eyes filled with tears. Whimpering, "No, no," she shook her head in disbelief.

"But, she is ready to go. She is ready to die."

A thought dropped into my heart, and I asked softly, "Marietta, what about you? Are you ready to die?"

"No," she said sadly. "No."

"Do you have a Bible?"

"I think so, let me check." She shuffled across the living room, down the hall. I heard her moving things in a bedroom; then, she came back and looked through a bookshelf in the hallway. She reached down to the bottom shelf and picked up a golden Gideon Bible she had taken from some hotel years before. She puffed the dust off the top and shuffled back to me.

I opened the Bible to Revelation 3:20 and paraphrased, "Jesus says, I'm standing at the door and knocking. If anyone hears my voice, and opens the door, I will come in and stay with him." I took Marietta's hand. "Jesus is here. Now. He is at the door of your heart. He is knocking, He wants to come in. Do you want to open the door and let Him in?"

"Yes," she nodded. We prayed a simple prayer of invitation. Marietta was radiant. "We have to tell Frieda," she exclaimed. "We have to let her know!"

Mom had tried for years to convince Marietta to give Jesus another chance—Marietta had been hurt years earlier by religious people. She was angry at the church and at God. She would never go to church with Mom or allow Mom to talk to her about God's love.

The next morning, Marietta rode with us to the hospital, where Joe drove us up to the front door. Marietta clasped my arm, and we shuffled into the lobby and toward the elevator. She clutched a milk-glass vase holding a single plastic rose. A very dusty, very large pink plastic rose.

Joe scooted a chair up close to Mom's bed. Marietta placed her rose on the side table, and then sat down on the chair. She reached for Mom's hand. The two old ladies clasped arthritic, knobby hands, veins prominent, tendons showing. "Frieda, I'll be there. I'll meet you in heaven."

"Oh, Marietta, I am so glad," tears ran down Mom's cheeks. "I am so glad."

"Frieda, will you wait for me? By the gate?"

Mom nodded, "I'll wait for you, Marietta; I'll meet you there."

After Marietta left, Mom whispered, "That's why I haven't died yet—Marietta."

The next day, I heard a commotion in the hallway. A nurse was saying very precisely, very loudly, "The-doctor-will-be-here-soon. He-will-let-you-know-the-results." I went out to investigate. On a gurney lay a small Hispanic lady, her eyes wide with fright, her lips trembling. I walked over, greeted her in Spanish, and asked the nurse if I could serve as interpreter.

Elisa had had a heart attack. Her husband, who spoke a little English, had gone home to get some things, and Elisa was being transferred to a room. I stayed with her; she would not let go of my hand even when they lifted her from the gurney to her bed. When things were calm and the nurses had left, I asked Elisa if I could pray with her. She nodded, "*Sí*." I prayed a simple, short prayer, thanking God for loving Elisa so much that He had arranged for her to be placed next to Mom so that I would be available to translate. When I finished praying, tears were streaming down Elisa's cheeks. "I have never heard a prayer like that before," she whispered. "I only know how to pray the rosary."

"Do you have a Spanish Bible?" I asked. She said they had one at home that someone had given to them. She had never read it, but she would ask her husband to bring it the next day.

I read Revelation 3:20 to Elisa. It is so beautiful in Spanish—Jesus is here at the door, He is knocking and wants to come in to have a meal with you, to stay with you. We prayed the sinner's prayer and Elisa looked at me, "I used to have Jesus in my head. Now I have him in my heart."

Her husband also received Christ. And Elisa told the dietician and a nurse from Panama about Jesus. They both accepted Jesus Christ as Savior.

Mom said softly, "That's why I haven't died yet."

***

I walked briskly to the nurses' station to ask why they were allowing so many visitors, mostly older ladies, to come to Mom's room. The nurse said, "I know there are too many visitors, but they all say they are her sister or her best friend." Throughout the years, Mom had visited every ladies' group in the county and even in the entire Panhandle of West Florida when she was District President of Women's Ministries.

When a woman would enter the room to visit "Sister Arnold," as they called her, I could see Mom "put on her ministry hat," calling the woman by name, asking about her family members by name. When the visitor left, Mom would sink back on the bed, exhausted.

Although Jan and I regretted having to do so, we finally had to restrict visitors.

Jan and I were with Mom late one afternoon when her heart stopped. As the monitor flat-lined, a nurse came running into the room, "Cough, Mrs. Arnold. Cough." Mom gave a small cough. The monitor beeped. "Cough, Mrs. Arnold. Cough!" Mom coughed again, twice, small coughs. The machine beeped twice and stopped. "Mrs. Arnold! Cough hard! *Now*! Cough hard!" Mom did, and her heart began to beat again.

A few minutes later Mom asked, "Where's Carl?" Jan said, as if she were speaking to a child, "Mom, you know Daddy is not here. He died several years ago." "Where's Carl?" Mom insisted. "Where is he? He was here just a few minutes ago. Here. Beside my bed," she motioned with her left hand. Jan and I looked at each other, asking with our eyes, "Do we tell her?" Jan nodded. I said, "Mom, your heart stopped. Three times. Your coughing brought you back to life." Mom smiled and nodded, "I knew it. I knew Carl was here!" Jan and I had not seen Daddy, but Mom surely thought she had.

After several days, Jan went home to get a good night's rest. I lay, sleeping fitfully, on a fold-out chair. About 3 a.m. Mom called very loudly, "Jesus! Jesus! Jesus!" I jumped out of bed and ran to her side. She was as white as a sheet. She was trembling and had broken out in a cold sweat.

"Margaret, pray! Plead the blood of Jesus. Pray!" I took her hand, her clasp was very tight. I began to pray. I quoted every Scripture I could remember. I felt the heavy oppression. Prayers seemed to bounce against the ceiling and plummet down to our feet, ineffective and leaden.

Mom's grasp tightened, her hand trembled. I prayed harder, "In the name of Jesus, I rebuke the demons of hell. I rebuke the power of Satan. Jesus is the Victor. Jesus is Lord." It seemed to me that I prayed for half-an-hour before the oppression lifted and our hearts filled with peace.

"Oh, Margaret," Mom said, her voice trembling, "I don't know if I was asleep or awake. I don't know if it was a dream or not. But a demon came. He came right here in front of me, on my chest. He held a document in one hand and a pen in the other. He sneered, 'Sign this document and denounce Christ. What is he doing for you now? He has deserted you. Sign here. Denounce him. He doesn't remember you. He has left you to suffer—alone! Sign here. Now!'"

That is when Mom had called out Jesus' name and begged for help to pray. It was all very real to her. Vivid. She said determinedly, "We have to tell the doctor. We have to tell Dr. Ziemba when he comes for his early morning rounds."

Mom would not let go of my hand, although I assured her we would tell the doctor when he came. I was honestly hoping she would forget about it, because I could only imagine a doctor listening to this story with derision.

She did not forget. As soon as the doctor entered, Mom squeezed my hand, "Tell him. Tell him."

I began the story, and as I did, the doctor looked closely at Mom. She would nod at various parts of the story and add details. The doctor pulled up a chair. He listened—intent on every word. I could not believe it.

When the story ended, Dr. Ziemba nodded his head, "I have seen this repeatedly. Satan never stops. He never gives up. Many Christians have told me similar stories."

Several nights later, Jan and I both stayed with Mom. Late into the night, Mom began to talk, "Just think ... when I get to heaven ...

I'll see Abraham ... and Isaac ... and Jacob ... and ..." with a huge sigh and dramatic flair, she moaned, "and poor ole Job." Jan and I burst out laughing—just as a nurse came in to check on Mom. Mom sensed the nurse's presence and said, loudly, "Here I am ... tryin' to die ... and you girls are giggling!" We laughed even harder. But the nurse did not—she glared at us—how dare we laugh when our Mom was dying!

The next day, the doctor explained that medical science could do nothing more. The nurse unhooked Mom from all the machines. We were just waiting for the end. Mom did not want any heroic measures. She was ready to go to heaven.

Mom became less and less responsive as the day wore on, and the nurse suggested that we call the family to come to the hospital; the end was near. That evening, Jan and Barry, Kim and Shawn and I sat around the bed, remembering good times and softly sharing stories. Mom's breathing slowed. And then, stopped.

After a few minutes, I said, "I'll go tell the nurse, so she can record the time of death." I walked down to the nurses' station and told the nurse, who was busy filling out paperwork. She nodded, jotted down the time of death, and said, "Take some time. Don't hurry. Say your good-byes."

I walked back to the room. We were all crying softly. After a while, Barry said, "I think I'll go down to the cafeteria and get a cup of coffee—it's gonna be a long night."

"Barry," I said quietly, "I brought a thermos of coffee. It hasn't even been opened—there, on the small table."

He walked over to the thermos, unscrewed the lid, poured coffee into a Styrofoam cup. The aroma of coffee filled the room.

A soft sound like someone clearing her throat came from the direction of the bed.

"Coffee ..." Mom said softly. "Coffee," she repeated, her voice more firm.

We could not believe it! She was alive!?

Barry brought his coffee cup over to the bedside. Jan gave Mom a sip—it was too hot and burned her lip. I said, "Well, I guess I'd better walk back to the nurses' station and tell them Mom is alive and drinking coffee!"

I walked down the hall and told the nurse. Matter-of-factly, she nodded and said, "I'll be right there."

A few minutes later, she walked briskly into the room, straight to Mom's side. The nurse reached for Mom's hand and said, "Mrs. Arnold, tell us about it. What was it like?"

It never occurred to us that Mom would have something to tell us—the nurse had experienced this before!

"Ohhh," Mom said softly, "You cannot imagine the feeling of peace. The tranquility. The joy. The lack of struggle. Oh, don't miss it. Don't miss it!"

"Did you see a light?" the nurse asked.

"I was on a path. In the distance, it was bright. Oh, the peace. The tranquility. The lack of struggle. You cannot imagine the joy. The tranquility."

During the next hours, Mom began to call out people's names, "Tell Melody Youngstrom. Jan, call Melody. Tell her not to miss it."

Jan went into the hallway and called Melody's Mom to get the phone number. Melody had grown up in the church, had rebelled against all things religious, and had moved out of town. Jan located her and relayed Mom's message.

The next day, a florist came bringing a beautiful bouquet of spring flowers. The card read, "I'll see you there, Melody."

Mom continued, "Barney. Call Barney Beasley." Big, burly policeman, sweet-but-defiant Barney, whose dad had been one of Daddy's deacons, came to the hospital, sat beside Mom and sobbed.

"That's why I haven't died yet," Mom affirmed.

Now, after this experience, Mom was even more eager to die. And on a Friday evening, she decided it was time. She called me over to her bedside. "How, exactly, do you die?" she asked.

"I'm not sure," I told her.

"How did Jesus die?" she asked. "What did He say, exactly?"

"Into thy hands I commit my spirit."

"Good," Mom said, squeezing my hand. "You pray it, and then I'll repeat it."

"Into thy hands … 'into thy hands' … I commit my spirit … 'I commit my spirit.'"

"Again," Mom insisted. "Into thy hands …." "Once more," she said. "Into thy hands …."

Mom nodded, satisfied. She would die now. Tonight.

Jan and I and Mom slept soundly. We all three awoke the next morning. Mom was not dead! And she was *not happy*. She had wanted to die. She was sure she would die that night. What did she do wrong? Why hadn't she died? God, surely, had forgotten all about her.

Disappointed, she was angry all day long. Her oatmeal was too cold. It didn't have enough sweeteners. The milk was warm. The coffee was cold. The air conditioner was too cold. Too hot. The bed was too high. Too low.

Finally, in the late afternoon, her anger changed to profound sadness. Tears rolled down her cheeks, "He has forgotten me. He didn't remember to come for me. I'm not that important. He has other things, more important things to do. He forgot all about me."

She drifted off to sleep.

Sunday morning dawned. Mom was quiet, sad. When the aide brought the breakfast tray, Jan began to uncover the dishes, as I reached for a colorful card propped open on the tray. It was a tract from the American Bible Society. I read aloud Isaiah 43:1-5:

> Do not be afraid—I will save you ... I have called you by name—you are mine. When you pass through deep waters, I will be with you; your troubles will not overwhelm you ... I am the Lord your God, the holy God of Israel, who saves you ... because you are precious to me and because I love you and give you honor. Do not be afraid—for I am with you.

Tears streamed down Mom's cheeks, "He didn't forget me. He remembers me. He knows my name."

Later that morning the phone rang. It was Crysti calling to check on Grandma and to apologize for not calling the last few days. "Both girls have been really sick with the chicken pox," she explained. "Their fever has broken now. They are over the worst of it."

Mom began to smile and nod her head, "That's why I haven't died yet—I want the girls to come to my funeral, and they wouldn't have been able to come. Tell Crysti to have the girls wear their

Easter dresses. Tell them to celebrate, because I will soon be 'One Happy Lady.'"

At noon, I tried to make Mom take one more bite of her Jello. She shook her head, "No! I can't gain any weight! I have to fit into my pretty, pink dress for my funeral."

Monday brought no change in Mom's condition. The doctor called Jan and me out into the hallway. "You need to consider which nursing home you want your Mom to go to. She is neither improving nor worsening. She will need to be transferred soon. I'll expect your answer tomorrow."

Jan and I were dismayed. Mom's prayer had been that she would not have to go to a nursing home. Through all her years of pastoral ministry, she had made hundreds of visits to pitiful patients in numerous, smelly nursing homes. Mom had told us to never, ever, put her in one, *please*. We did not tell Mom what the doctor said.

In the afternoon, Mom said, "Margaret, do you see them?"

"See who?"

"Them, the people in here. I'm not crazy. They're here. You don't see them? Look over there by the door—there is Sister Jernigan ... and Julia Blanton, and next to her is Sister Hanks ... and Brother Majors." Mom gestured across the room, calling by name people who had died long before, people she had not mentioned in years. Near the foot of her bed, she indicated, "Oh, there's Mark!" I knew Mark; he was a pastor's son who had drowned as a toddler in a swimming pool. "Mom! How big is Mark? How tall is he?"

Mom waved her hand. "It doesn't matter, that's not important." She kept on, scanning the room and calling out the names of people she saw.

Then tears filled her eyes, "I didn't know it would be like this. I knew I would be happy to go. But I didn't know they would come to welcome me. It's like a surprise birthday party."

She continued, "And of course Carl is here," she motioned to the side of the bed. "He's always here now. And so is this one up here beyond my shoulder, by my head."

"Who is that? Up by the head of your bed?" I wanted to know.

"I'm not sure. But he's always there now. I think it must be my guardian angel."

I was fascinated to watch Mom's transition into the spirit world, the blending of the natural and the eternal.

Later that night, toward morning, Mom cried out in pain, "Oh, my leg! My leg!"

We called the nurse, who looked at Mom's thigh and then gave her one Tylenol.

When the doctor made his rounds, he sent Mom for x-rays. He called Jan and me into the hallway, once again, with the results. "Mrs. Arnold threw a clot—a large clot, in her right thigh. It is positioned in the artery where it divides to serve the back and the front of the leg. There is no circulation in her leg at this time. Without an operation to remove the clot, gangrene will set in. But, if we operate, your mother will die on the operating table, because her heart is not strong enough for surgery. However, if we do not operate, she will die of gangrene, and that is an excruciatingly painful death. You must decide what to do. I will be back in a few minutes for your answer."

Jan and I looked at each other. "Mom would want to know the truth," Jan said. We walked back into Mom's room. "What did he say?" she questioned immediately. Jan and I looked at each other again. We nodded. We told her the truth.

Mom began to smile, even before we had finished the details of the severity of her condition. She sighed, and with a wide smile whispered, "Good, oh good. This is what God will use to take me home. Good."

Throughout the day the pain increased in her leg. The nurse came into the room toward evening to give Mom a shot of morphine. Mom looked up, saw the needle and asked, "Is that habit forming?" Even the cranky nurse had to smile this time.

A little while later Mom exclaimed, "My teeth! We need to clean my teeth." Jan and I looked at each other. Jan said, "Excuse me, but I don't do teeth."

I reached for some gloves, and then reached for Mom's teeth. She helped me remove the upper plate and her lower "bridge" and plop them into the curved, pink plastic tray. I went to the sink and brushed Mom's teeth. She helped me put them back in place. "Ah," she sighed as she rubbed her tongue over the clean surface, "I couldn't go to heaven with dirty teeth."

A few hours passed. The phone rang. It was Joe. We talked quietly for a few minutes and I walked back to the bed.

"Is he coming tonight?" Mom asked.

"No, Mom. He can't get here tonight, it's too far –"

Mom interrupted, "Not Joe. Jesus. Is He coming tonight?

"Yes. Yes ... He's coming tonight."

Crying quietly, Jan and I stood on each side of the bed holding Mom's hands. I said softly, "Suffering may endure for a night but joy comes in the morning."

Mom nodded. I repeated, "Suffering ... may endure ... for a night ... but joy comes in the morning."

A little while later, Mom asked softly, "Is it morning yet?"

"Almost, Mom, almost."

She took a shallow breath, her last. And in that quiet moment she left us, to go to heaven, accompanied by Daddy and her guardian angel and her friends.

My brother flew in from Houston. He had long ago left behind his childhood religion. "We'll just have a brief funeral service at the funeral home," he said.

Jan, who was usually non-confrontational (being the middle child), stood up to David. "No. We will have the funeral at the Brownsville church."

David smiled, "There will be about a half-dozen old ladies at this funeral. It will be embarrassing in that big auditorium."

We held the funeral at Brownsville Assembly of God. The large auditorium was full.

My Aunt Jo and Uncle Mac Arnold came from Illinois. So did Ed and Mary Bernreuter, whom God had used to provide shoes in answer to my prayer as a five-year old little girl starting school in Nashville, Illinois. Dr. Ziemba came, as well as several of the nurses. Elisa was there with her Spanish family.

Crysti's girls, Jennifer and Kyndal, wore their colorful Easter dresses—with chicken pox spots shining through.

Pastor John Kilpatrick spoke about finishing the race, and then he led the congregation in the sinner's prayer. He concluded, "We did not come here to grieve, we came to celebrate—because today, in her own words, Frieda Arnold is 'One Happy Lady!'"

Jennifer and Kyndal ready for the funeral

"JESUS MAKES BAD PEOPLE GOOD."
"JESUCRISTO CONVIERTE A LOS MALOS EN BUENOS."

28

Carol

I'm from Bart-tow, Florida.

Carol Young, southern drawl defining her heritage, ran camera on our trip to Guatemala and performed a thousand other technical duties there. At the STAR studio, as engineer, she kept all the video and audio running. Her quick smile and quirky sense of humor endeared her not only to us older missionaries, but also to the young missionary volunteers, including Paula Atkinson, (who made us laugh on the bus in Guatemala).

Carol Young on a rooftop in South America

In those days, before digital video, equipment was "linear." And very expensive. Dozens of pieces of equipment filled countertops, and large racks held supporting technical machines. Miles of cable (it seemed) connected everything, back behind the racks.

Day in and day out, Carol and Joe talked tech-y stuff, such as how to upgrade our equipment on a shoe-string budget and how to get a few more hundred hours out of the video duplication machines.

Carol Young, engineer on a shoe-string budget
(in the early days of STAR, before the control room was completed)

***

Now that other missionaries in other countries saw the value of television programming and began to need video equipment and production facilities, Joe and Carol pondered and reasoned and bounced ideas around, such as "What if we could somehow combine our resources?"

Day after day, Joe envisioned what a combined facility should resemble. He researched production equipment.

And then, in September 1987, he disappeared to his office where he began to type up a proposal entitled, "Foreign Missions Media Center." He stated:

> In the Division of Foreign Missions, there has been much thought, talk, planning, and work toward implementing the communications tools God has given us ... These

new evangelistic tools did not come with operational manuals for foreign missions work. We are writing them! ... God asks that we be good stewards. We cannot furnish every missionary with media equipment with today's prices and ever-advancing technology ...

I will endeavor to set down in this paper my thoughts as to a viable option of implementing the media in reaching our world in our generation. Through talking with others, reading, and being involved in a media ministry for the past thirteen years, the following media center strategy has formed. I am not claiming that it is without error. It will probably need much change, refinement, and adjustment before becoming usable. I present this paper hoping that it can become at least the beginning of a meaningful strategy for the utilization of the media tools, personnel, and facility resources available to us.

Tampa International Airport Model ....

Joe went on to describe the actual Tampa Airport design—a central hub with spokes radiating from it. The central hub contains ticket counters, luggage check-in and retrieval, restaurants and gift shops: things common to all passengers. The outlying spokes house the individual airlines' departure and arrival gates.

Joe compared video production needs: about ten percent of the time is actually spent in the studio to film, while ninety percent of the time consists of pre-production and post-production—making the plans, and then editing the video and audio clips together.

On October 7, 1987, Joe presented his proposal to the Foreign Missions Committee. What if all video-missionaries shared a "hub," a state-of-the-art studio where professional camera operators filmed in various languages? Then, each producer could retire to his own "spoke"—offices and editing suites. The savings in missions' dollars would be tremendous. "We're all struggling for the same thing," Joe reasoned. "We need missions' offerings and talented volunteers. What if we shared the 'pool'?"

Joe reported to the STAR staff, "The committee accepted the concept without reservation. Rev. Hogan told me that this was the answer he had struggled for. The only snag is that our central headquarters is talking of a media center in Springfield. I told them we would be happy to cooperate with that. It could be the hub, and we could have our editing facilities in adjacent buildings." Joe told us not to plan any more growth in our facilities in Florida because plans were pending for a possible move.

Days passed. No word yet on where or when to begin combining efforts. Weeks passed. Joe called headquarters, "Yes, yes. We want to do this. It is a wonderful idea to share resources."

Months passed. And we eventually realized that it would not happen. Carol patched equipment and soldered connections; we scheduled missionary services to recruit additional volunteers; and we made phone calls, continuing to raise money to repair worn-out equipment.

***

Joe's focus seemed inevitably to be centered on the challenge of "lack of equipment, lack of personnel, lack of funds." Yet, despite these constant challenges, God provided just enough, just at the precise time, just the person we needed!

A letter to our donors during that period included these facts:

1. Today there are twenty-five full-time people on the STAR team.

2. Radio and television programming is used in fifty-one countries of the world: as far away from Latin America as Africa and India.

3. Many churches have been started with the use of video cassettes of STAR programming.

4. Political leaders have been "softened up" by their families watching Bobo and the *Secret Place* puppets.

5. National television stations have placed the program on the air free of charge in sixteen different areas of Latin America.

6. Seventeen cable and broadcast television outlets release *Secret Place* and/or *Lugar Secreto* here in the United States.

7. Response is constant from the children who write to say they have been born again or greatly blessed by watching the programs.

8. A total of over 60,000 audio and television programs have been distributed since STAR began.

Dear Bobo,

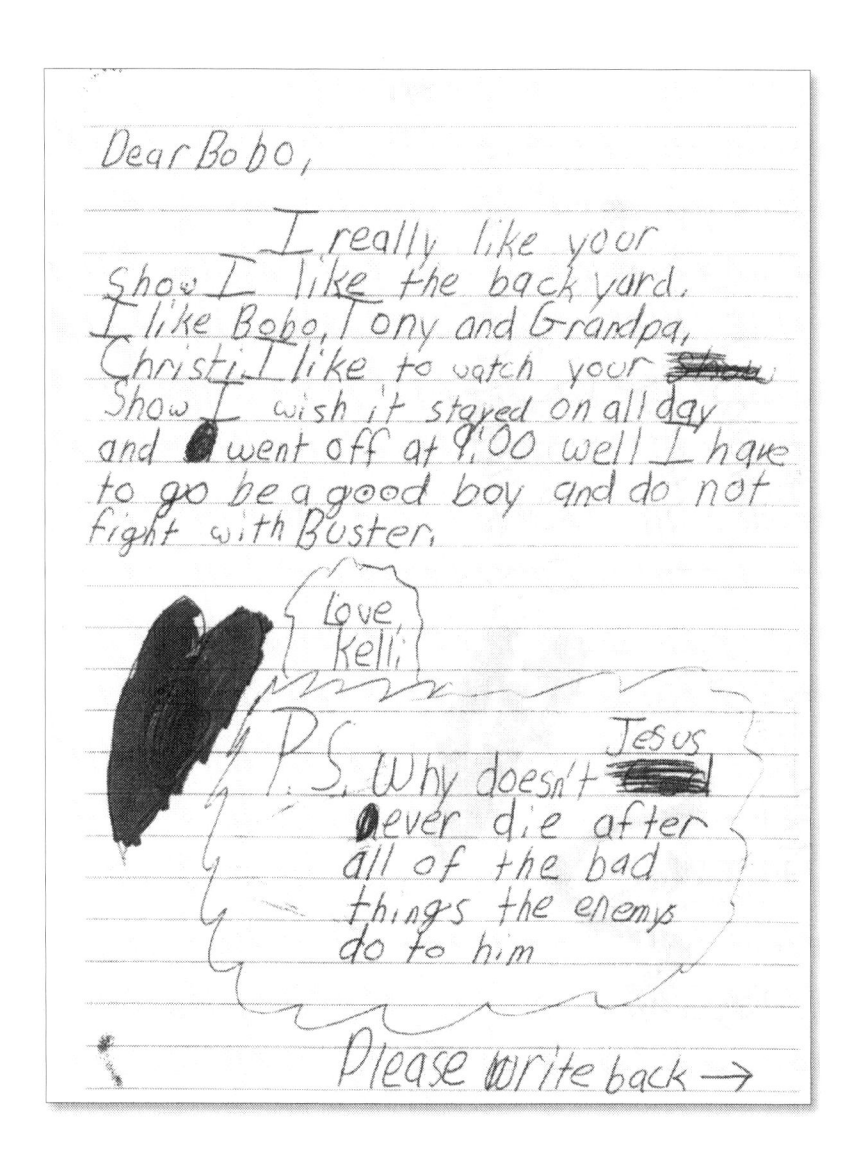

I really like your show. I like the back yard. I like Bobo, Tony and Grandpa, Christi. I like to watch your show. I wish it stayed on all day and went off at 9:00 well I have to go be a good boy and do not fight with Buster.

love,
Kelli

P.S. Why doesn't Jesus ever die after all of the bad things the enemys do to him

Please write back →

A Place for People, Puppets, and Cockroach Soup

"MEMORIZE THE BIBLE VERSE ON THE NEXT PAGE!"
"¡MEMORIZA EL VERSICULO BIBLICO DE LA SIGUIENTE PAGINA!"

29

Isaac

Am I going to die?

> If you want a happy ending,
> That depends, of course,
> On where you stop your story.
> –*Orson Welles*

I clearly remember the day things began to change—events were set in motion that none of us could foresee.

Our missions director flew to Florida and came to our house. Joe and I sat in our living room on the old brown couch, as the director asked, "Joe, do you want STAR to remain a 'Mom and Pop' endeavor? Do you want to hold it back with you and Margaret leading it? Or do you want STAR to expand? To become greater than yourselves?"

Joe responded immediately, "I do not want to stand in the way of what God wants to do."

"Then, you are no longer in charge of STAR. I will put in place a committee of missionaries. They will govern. You will be on the committee, of course, but as just another member."

Thus, new missionaries came. Good men; but men who did not have our vision. They had not fought to get every puppet, every prop, every square foot of office space and studio building. These men stepped on board while the train sped rapidly down the rail. They settled in comfortably and formulated wise plans.

STAR must become a business, they reasoned. In fact, in order not to offend vendors or potential investors or clients, the name must be changed from *STAR Ministries* to *STAR Communications*. And so, office space was expanded by building a second floor over the existing 30'x50' building. The duplication area was expanded to 20'x30'; it backed up to a new puppet storage room. A two-story prop storage area gave ample and wonderful space. The original 30'x50' metal "skin" was removed from inside the new structure, reassembled out back, and became a wonderful carpenter's shop. STAR now occupied 20,000 square feet.

Distribution flourished. A new regional boss was appointed. He told us that *Lugar Secreto* was passé, that there was no place for puppets in ministry. We should begin to produce only Christian educational programs for adults.

And so, *poco a poco* (little by little), the camel took over the tent. Children's emphasis slid to the side. Fees must be charged for the video tapes. We needed to be worldly wise, not so naïve and childish as to give away products.

I began to feel like an outsider in my own office. I grieved that there seemed to be little place for puppets, for children's ministry, in this newly morphed *STAR Communications*. Missionaries with no video experience positioned themselves in charge of productions.

The following summer, Joe and I attended the School of Missions in Missouri. In conversation with Paul Hutsell, whom we had first met when we served as missionaries in Paraguay, Paul said, "If you ever leave STAR, I wish you would come to Ecuador. I'm Area Director there now, and we have hundreds of new converts who really need Bible teaching."

A way of escape! Should we go? This was not the first time I had felt overwhelmed at STAR. Someone asked me one time if we ever had any tensions at STAR. I wonder if we ever did *not*. We worked on split-second timing, editing and shooting day after day after day. The production schedule, coupled with the spiritual burden, sat heavily on our shoulders.

At one point during this period, Crysti went into the dressing room to put on her *Lugar Secreto* costume-dress. She came back out, grinning, saying, "OK, who took my dress? 'Fess up. It's time to get out on the set."

No one responded. Crysti had expected laughter and a funny confession. But no one "confessed" to having taken the dress from where it had been hanging a few hours earlier. We knew no staff member would have done such a thing, but we had a number of summer interns. We searched the rest rooms. We searched the office area. We searched the studio, the control room, the puppet room, the props room. Nothing. We looked in the trash cans, in the dumpster.

An old dormitory belonging to the church was adjacent to the studio, and several of our summer volunteers were housed in it. We searched every square inch of the dorm. Nothing. We reassembled back in the studio, forlorn and sobered. What could we do? We had already shot the "openings" with Crysti wearing the costume-dress; the segments we needed to shoot were the continuation of the same shows, the "closings."

Suddenly, Evelyn remembered that a young woman had worn an identical dress to her church the previous Sunday. Evelyn called the woman, who immediately left work, went home, picked up her dress, and brought it to the studio. It was one size larger, but Crysti was pregnant at the time, so the dress fit perfectly! We never discovered who had "stolen" Crysti's dress; but, thank God, He provided another one!

Another distressing time that I especially remember is when a woman, a volunteer, caused heart-breaking dissension among the staff. Like a bumblebee, she went from person to person with her poisonous pollen. Then, after several tumultuous months at STAR, she and her husband, who was a good construction worker, went to the Native American Bible College, where she caused such chaos that people resigned in tears.

Missionaries, generally speaking, are their own bosses. They have to be independent in order to sacrifice everything, leave home, and persevere for months while raising their monetary support. But a group of them together ... (smile) ... watch out! They tend not to be subservient to other missionaries. Then, when you mix in the volunteers—each one knows best and many will tell you so, vehemently, without hesitation.

Sometimes, the situation becomes volatile. As the director, Joe had great responsibility without any authority. He could neither hire nor fire. Each missionary had just as much "pull" with our headquarters personnel as Joe did. Once, Joe called our boss regarding a missionary who scheduled his vacation right in the middle of a major video production. Our boss replied, "He can take his vacation whenever he wants."

We knew that we fought a spiritual battle. The apostle Paul writes often of the spiritual struggle each Christian endures. And, being on the front lines of evangelism, touching so many thousands of lives, we became ideal targets of the Adversary-Satan. Patiently, and not-so-patiently, we worked through each crisis. Some battles we fought, some we waited out, some we lost. But always we marched forward.

Besides the STAR "battles," personal growth caused pain, too. In 1985 Tim called from Evangel College, "Mom, you have to buy a book our psychology professor recommends, *Happiness is a Choice* by Minirth and Meier. It explains so much!"

I bought the book and began to read it so that I could "help others." But as I read the introduction, I was hit with an unwanted truth: many ministers and missionaries are so self-sacrificing that they become martyrs to the detriment of their own families. The authors questioned my motives, analyzed my obsessive-compulsive behavior, and, generally, turned me upside down. I cried, and grew, and read some more. I kept the book alongside my Bible for several years, reading in both books daily.

I knew the truths applied to me, to us. We felt we had to raise funds. We visited churches all over Florida. Everyone received us graciously and gave generously. Many weekends, after the children were grown and gone from home, Joe and I left the studio headed to a weekend missions' convention. A Friday night banquet, Saturday morning breakfast, Saturday evening small group, Sunday school class, Sunday morning services (both adult and children's), and Sunday evening service. We drove back to the studio on Monday morning, exhausted and ready to begin another week. With our win-the-world-for-Jesus-now mindset, how could we do differently?

And so, the years of tension took their toll. Our bodies grew tired. Our spirits became weary from the ten-year struggle. Maybe we should have stayed and fought for control. Maybe we suffered from burnout and should have backed off to rest for a few weeks. I don't know. But, we resigned from STAR effective January, 1988, itinerated for a year, and moved to Ecuador in January, 1989.

In Quito, Paul Hutsell found for us a tiny apartment located on the fifth floor of his office building. An easy chair faced a very large picture window that looked toward the towering volcano, *Pichincha*.

***

I sat in the chair, day after day, facing the mountain, reading my Bible, praying. I pictured Abraham taking Isaac to be sacrificed. Isaac, his son, his only son, the son he dearly loved, the son God himself gave to Abraham. This precious son became Abraham's sacrifice.

I saw Abraham walking to the top of the mountain where he and Isaac piled stones to make an altar. Abraham said, "Son, lie down here, on top of the rock pile. Hold still; let me put this leather cord around your hands and your ankles." Isaac is patient, not understanding what is happening. Abraham raises the knife. Ready. Willing to sacrifice his beloved son. Maybe Isaac asks, "Dad, what are you doing? Am I going to die?" Then, suddenly, God intervenes. A ram stands nearby, caught in the bushes. Isaac is restored to his father.

I sat in my armchair. I looked out my window at the volcano, the mountain. I climbed up. High. I piled stones for an altar. I placed STAR, our precious child, on the altar. I raised the knife. "Intervene, God," I prayed. "Stop this sacrifice of the 'son' you gave us." I paused. I waited. I waited to hear God's voice. I waited for God to intervene, to restore STAR to its original vision. I waited for the phone to ring, to call us back.

Day after day, I climbed the mountain. Day after day, I held the knife over our beloved Isaac-STAR, and prayed for God to intervene. But there was no answer. God remained silent. And STAR died. STAR died to me. STAR died to Joe. And STAR itself died. After about a year, the missions board closed it down, leaving a radio remnant. I cannot say why. I cannot say that becoming *STAR Communications* instead of *STAR Ministries* is why. I cannot say that because the sparkle who is *Bobo* was dampened day by day, the fire died. I just know that I was heartbroken.

***

The year we spent in Ecuador was therapeutic and restful. Toward the end of that year, I finally let go of my grief. One day as I read Daniel, chapter 4:28-37, I identified with Nebuchadnezzar. I read about his pride, about his being shocked by God's actions, and his dawning understanding of God's sovereignty.

In verse 32, God says to Nebuchadnezzar, "You will be driven away from people ... until you acknowledge that the Most High is sovereign over the kingdoms of men and gives them to anyone he wishes." And verse 35, "He does as he pleases with the powers of heaven and the peoples of the earth. No one can hold back his hand or say to him: 'What have you done?'"

After many days, I was able to pray, with Nebuchadnezzar, verse 37, "Now I ... praise and exalt and glorify the King of heaven, because everything he does is right and all his ways are just. And those who walk in pride he is able to humble."

Some weeks later, still re-reading the same chapter, I paused when I read Daniel 4:15. Nebuchadnezzar's tree would be cut down because of his pride; however, God said, "But let the stump and its roots, bound with iron and bronze, remain in the ground, in the grass of the field." I was just a stump now. But my roots remained. My roots dug deeper than ever into the soil of God's Sovereignty. Would the stump ever sprout again? Only God knew.

Lord Jesus, I want to be best friends. I have done wrong things. I have thought and said bad things, too. I am sorry. Please forgive me. I do not want to do them again. Come into my heart and teach me. Amen.

THIS PRAYER WILL HELP YOU BE GOD'S CHILD...

A Place for People, Puppets, and Cockroach Soup

THE BIBLE SAYS, "Give thanks in all things."
LA BIBLIA DICE: "Da gracias a Dios por todo."

30

Maggie

Can a person change her name?

1992

After a recuperative year in Ecuador, Joe and I returned to the States, where, for the following three years, we taught in a Bible college, and then accepted a pastorate at a church. We felt that we failed at both. We were square pegs in round holes.

We had been really excited to be invited to the college, to build a television production studio and teach communications classes. We could pass on to the students, to the next generation, all the skills and passion we had acquired to do television and radio production, including the teaching of puppeteering and specialized set building. I developed a notebook entitled *Production Techniques* and filled it with practical tips, check-lists, and step-by-step procedures. But ... the circumstances under which we had been hired changed drastically when the conceptualization of the studio was taken out of our hands and placed under different administration.

So, sitting on our hands and unable to proceed in any meaningful way, we resigned. It was heart-wrenching to leave the students, but thankfully, we were able to take a group on a trip to Central America. (Years later we learned that the experience crystallized the call to missions for several of the students, including Rennae and Nelson DeFreitas.)

Joe, Bobo, and Margaret in San Salvador

Bobo, Joe, and Staci Innskeep at a
Castillo del Rey rally, El Salvador

What could we do now? We had given up our foreign missions appointment to become professors. However, we were ministers, above all, so we began to look for a church to pastor.

Once again, we were excited—this time to move to a small town in central Florida as pastors. Joe preached on evangelism, witnessing to your neighbors, bringing people to church with you. The church began to grow. But one deacon told Joe, "You make me feel under conviction. I just want to feel good when I come to church."

We should have taken the clue! By the following year, the "establishment" grew angry because of all the new people who were now attending the church. The power base had shifted, and the church stood on the verge of a split. To avoid that, we resigned on a Sunday morning even as we broke attendance records. We did not want the new people to become disillusioned, and we hoped a different pastor could bridge the gap. He did, and the church flourishes today.

Twenty years later, one of our youth from that church found us on Facebook. Steven Sellars wrote,

> You and Joe both played such a major role in my life. Thank you so much. This is my last Sunday as pastor of this church after 14 years. And I think of how thankful I am to even be here ... doing what I am doing. And it all started because a pastor and his wife took the time to disciple me; to provide spiritual care for me; and to kick me in the pants so I would leave home for Bible College (smile). You both will always be at the root of my life when God took over. Being a firefighter, an EMT, a Pastor and soon a professional counselor to EMTs is the coolest thing I could ever think of doing in life. I am so blessed to have the opportunity to provide care for heroes. Now if I can find a career that pays! ha-ha. Anyway, thank you so much!! I love you both!

But, all those years earlier, when we left that church, we had no place to go, no job, no income, no place to live, no place to belong.

I had already experienced deep pain—when I was in childbirth; when we lived in Temuco, Chile; when we left *STAR Communications*. But this was not just pain. This was character identity. This was the end of my life as I knew it.

We were homeless. We were unemployed. We had some savings, which would soon be depleted. We could see ourselves, totally bankrupt, living on the street as utter and complete failures. What could we "do" if we were not ministers or missionaries? That's all we had ever been.

Tim said, "Come stay with us. My wife and I will make room here in Lakeland, in our tiny apartment." So, Joe and I lugged our suitcases up a twisting flight of stairs to Tim's extra room which housed: our old brown couch! The hide-a-bed was still as uncomfortable as ever. We hit our knees and shins on the side hinges; and through the thin mattress, our bottoms bounced off the metal bars. But it was inside. Inside, under a roof. And it was near Lake Hollingsworth.

The next morning, Tim said, "Lots of people like to walk around the lake."

So, Joe and I began to walk. Joe promised to go back and get the car if I couldn't make it all three miles around the lake. But I made it—just barely. Day after day we walked. We cried. We prayed. We despaired. I kept re-hashing all of our failures. Days filled with gloom. Nights brought negative thoughts preying in the darkness, then springing to torment us as we tossed and turned.

I spiraled downward into burnout, and during those dark days I began to write. Five months later, a tiny door opened a tiny crack, to give us a tiny hope of a new, totally different ministry. Pastor Bob Newman offered Joe a job as principal of Beacon Christian Academy. Bob asked me to become Daycare Director.

THE BURNOUT SPIRAL
My journey

Sometimes I call it burnout.
Sometimes I call it pride.
Probably it is both.
Maybe burnout is caused by pride.

I didn't know I had spiritual pride.
I didn't mean to.
I didn't intend to burn out.
I just wanted to work for God. To bring in the harvest.

To win souls—as many as possible, as efficiently as possible, as quickly as possible.

Of course, I am inferior. But I remember that "I can do all things through Christ":
I can do it.
I must do it.
If I don't, who will?
God called me to do it.
Hurry. The world needs this.
Let's get bigger.
Let's get better.
Wow, God is sure using me!
Hurry now.
Bigger. More. Better. Larger. Expand this ministry.
Don't slow me down.
God called me to do this. Out of my way. Help, don't hinder.
Jump on this train. Hurry.

God, they're slowing me down.
God, they don't understand.
You called me.
How can you let them hinder me?
Lord, they're dragging their feet.
Lord! Don't let them slow me down.
God, this is your work.
You are blessing me. I'm doing a wonderful job.
If it weren't for these people hindering me, we could reach the world.
God, help.
God, don't let them do this to me.
God?
God, where are you?

OK. I'll try this ministry over here.
Here, I can proceed with what God called me to do.
Yeah.
All right. Let's go.
What? Too fast?

Wait a minute, Mister. God called me.
God gave me these ideas.
Back off.
Don't hinder God's work.
Um.
OK. Nice try. We'll move again.
God, do you see what they are doing to me?
God?
God, where are you?

New assignment. New place. New push.
Tired, this time.
But God will help me. I think.
Push. God called me. Push. Hurry.
Come on. Jump on the train. God called me.
Go. Go. Do. Achieve. Hurry.
God, they're starting to hinder me.
Again.
Lord, they're dragging their feet.
Again.
Lord, do something.
Stop them from hindering your work.
Don't you see them, Lord?
Why don't you do something?
Lord, they're pushing me out.
God, I have no place to go.
Lord, where are you?
I've worked for you.
I've given my life for you.
I've done great things for you.
Why are you letting this happen to me?
God?
God, where are you?
God
    Where
        Are
            You
                ??????????

Bottom.
Below bottom.
Sinking.
Drowning.
Suffocating.
Flat on my face, in the mud, at the foot of the cross.
Mud from Jesus' blood. Mud from Jesus' tears. Mud from my own tears.

Do you love me, Lord? Even when I fail?
Do you love me, Lord, even now?
Do you care?
Do you?
Do you?

What?
What are you saying?
You do?
You do?
I don't have to work for your love?
You love me?
<u>You</u> love me.
You <u>love</u> me.
You love <u>me</u>.

Relax. Breathe deeply. Rest. Be.
Be.
Be. Wait. Easy now.
No reputation.
Jesus, you made yourself of no reputation.

Just be.
Be ready. Ready to give an answer.
Be witnesses. Not *do* witnessing.
Be love. Be available to love.
Care about each individual.
Care about each person I meet.
Stop and listen.
Truly listen. To each person.

Not task oriented anymore.
Jesus, am I getting to know you?
Am I sharing in your suffering?
Rejection. Emotional pain. Loneliness. Disappointment. Lack of God's intervention.
Failure in everyone's eyes, but God's.
Misunderstood. Object of gossip. Betrayed.
Loved by Jesus Christ.
Accepted by Jesus Christ.
Pruned by Jesus Christ.
Disciplined by Jesus Christ.

Content now. Not striving.
Being now. Not doing.
Available now, not storming the ramparts.
Loving now, not demanding.
Remembering people—not tasks.

Days pass. Weeks pass. Months pass.
A door.
An open door.
For me?
A place to "be"?
A place to minister, not to "do" ministry?
A place to love individual people?
A place to stop and listen.
Listen to your quiet voice, Jesus.
Listen to each person you place in my path.

An insignificant place.
Ah, but not to you, Lord.
No ministry is small to you, Lord.
No place is unimportant to you, Lord.

Oh! I see you move again, Jesus!
There is joy mixed with my tears.
Joy!
Thank you, Lord.
Thank you for breaking me.

Thank you for crushing me.
Thank you for loving me.
Lives are being changed.
I'm not striving to "do."
I'm just "being."
You are shining through me.
Oh, thank you, Jesus.

Transparent.
Open.
No hidden agenda.
No power struggle.
Beyond faith.
Beyond faith to trust.
Trust.

***

As I walked, slowly, through this process, I realized that I did not want to be called *Margaret*—my old self. Self-righteous and proud. Driven to excel. I wanted to be *Maggie*—a softer me, more reliant on God's timing, more knowledgeable of God's sovereignty, more dependent on God's grace.

Being director of Beacon Preschool and Afterschool care at Trinity Assembly of God fulfilled me in a way I could not have imagined. I loved all thirty of my teachers. I loved the children. Parents came to me with their problems. I held unruly children as they cried, wounded by problems in their home. Teachers in tears poured out their hearts to me. Amazingly, I became a true servant of Jesus Christ without even trying!

But sometimes I thought of the stump … with its roots in the ground. If anyone asked me who I was, I replied without even thinking, "I'm a missionary." That was who I was. That is who I am, my core. Would the stump ever sprout again?

Joe, Maggie, Bobo

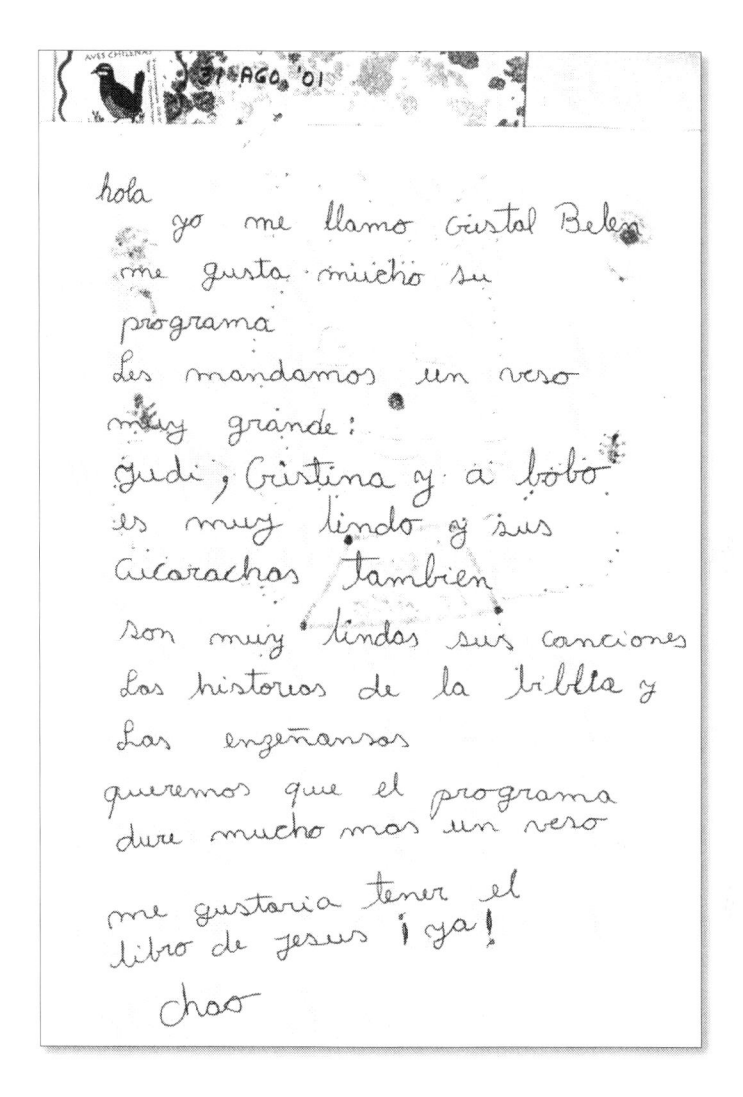

> hola
> yo me llamo Cristal Belen
> me gusta mucho su programa
> Les mandamos un beso muy grande:
> Judi, Cristina y a bobo
> es muy lindo y sus cucarachas tambien
> son muy lindas sus canciones
> Las historias de la biblia y las enzeñansas
> queremos que el programa dure mucho mas un beso
> me gustaria tener el libro de Jesus ¡ ya!
> chao

"Hello, my name is Cristal and I really like your program. I send a great big kiss to Judy, Cristina and Bobo. He is really cute and so are his *cucarachas*. The songs are very good, so are the Bible stories and the teachings. We hope the program will go on for a very long time. A kiss. I would like the book about Jesus, right now! Bye"

A Place for People, Puppets, and Cockroach Soup

ROSIE'S BEST FRIEND IS JESUS.
CRISTO ES EL MEJOR AMIGO DE ROSITA.

Gene and Jeanne

From here to the world

Mother's Day, May 10, 2009

Missionaries Gene and Jeanne LaMay, their arms loaded with DVDs, walked up the steps beside the platform at Victory Church, Lakeland, Florida. I followed. Nexi descended toward us. Her eyes glistened with joy. Her smile broadened.

"*¡Te acordaste!*" she exclaimed. "You remembered!"

Five days before, in Orlando, Joe and I had met Nexi and the twenty-one other members of the Cuban Chorale. They had traveled from Cuba with their Superintendent, Hector Hunter, along with missionary interpreter Daniel Arizarry. They had come to Florida at the request of District Missions Director Dan Betzer, in order to help raise funds for ministry in Cuba, Betzer's 2009 missions project for Peninsular Florida.

Standing at a reception for the Betzers, Joe and I began to converse with the Cubans. Tentatively, I asked, "Have you ever heard of the television program *Lugar Secreto*?"

Nexi's face lit up, "*¿Lugar Secreto? Claro que sí –con Bobito y Cristina.*" (Of course, with Bobo and Cristina.)

"I'm the producer of that show. Joe operates the puppet *Bobo*," I told her in Spanish.

You would have thought I'd announced that a celebrity had just arrived! Nexi turned to the group and proclaimed in a loud voice, "*¡Oye! Bobo está aquí, ¡del Lugar Secreto!*"

The Cubans gathered around Joe. "Talk," they said, "We want to hear Bobo!"

They laughed and laughed! As delighted as children, they mimed, word for word, various scenes in the shows. They surrounded Joe to take photos with the person who "was" Bobo.

They explained, then, that years ago, someone had smuggled into Cuba a few VHS video cassettes. They had played the tapes over and over and over again until you could hardly see the video.

We asked if they owned DVD players, and if so, would they like to have *Lugar Secreto* on DVD?

Oh yes! That would be wonderful! They began counting to see how many churches they were representing—eight, they decided. Could they have sets of DVDs for eight churches?

And now, with Gene and Jeanne, I stood poised to hand over the DVDs. Eight sets of fifty-two programs plus a Teacher's Manual on CD. Also on CD, the *Lugar Secreto* coloring book with sketches of the puppet characters.

"My sister is head of the Sunday School department for our section," exclaimed Nexi. "She will distribute these to many churches!"

Jeanne handed Nexi another packet of six DVDs: *El Nuevo Lugar Secreto*: programs for adolescents with themes on AIDS, Slander, and Unforgiveness.

"I teach adolescents," murmured Nexi with tears.

Then Gene handed her even more DVDs: *Un Encuentro con Dios (Meet God!)* with the Teacher's Manual on CD. Also for adolescents, with Dan Betzer as host.

Nexi began handing the packets to members of the Chorale. They unzipped the packets to gaze at their treasures. They could hardly believe they were receiving this tremendous blessing for Cuba. Their eyes glistened with tears.

Nexi clasped the DVDs to her heart. "*Gracias. Mil gracias,*" she whispered, her eyes brimming with tears. "Thank you. A thousand times thank you."

***

Yes, Joe and I *did* return to STAR. We were reappointed as missionaries in 1994, and lived for a year in Colombia to help the national church with television productions.

Colombia, TV Production Class

Then, from a stump and from smoldering ashes, we formed a new *STAR Media Ministries* in 1996.

Gradually, another wonderful group of volunteers and short-term missionaries came to join us.

Roland and Evelyn Blount had remained in a small section of the STAR building to facilitate radio productions.

In the audio studios, Jerónimo Pérez and his family recorded *Radio Avance*. These radio programs for the "Decade of Harvest" reached into every Latin American country and touched tens of thousands of lives. We were honored to share the building with Pastor Jerónimo.

Once again, the Peninsular Florida District embraced us.

Pastors opened their churches to us, and church members volunteered for hundreds of tasks from sewing to mowing.

The new *STAR Media Ministries* Team

***

During the next few years we would:

1. Produce programming for adolescents, an audience we had not targeted earlier.
2. Conduct workshops and seminars, both in-house and also on location.
3. Host interns and short-term missionary associates.
4. Produce additional *Vecinitos* radio programs.
5. Write bilingual scripts and produce audio CDs for short-term missions groups to use with puppets or as pantomimes in street ministry.
6. Produce promotional videos for sister ministries.
7. Make possible John and Mary Ann Wilkie's dream of a video Bible Institute.
8. Upgrade and digitize our classic *Lugar Secreto* and educational programs.

The entire STAR building was returned to us. Our missions organization donated equipment and supplies through Speed-the-Light, Light for the Lost, Boys and Girls Missionary Crusades. The new, smaller, more efficient equipment, studio lights, and cameras made productions professional (and fun).

Cast and Crew of the new pilot production, puppets included

Fredda made dozens of new puppets, even better ones, and we combined them with our "regulars" that each puppeteer had taken home and guarded jealously.

A few of Fredda's new puppet creations

Carlos, Judy, Steve, Sarita, Maritza
holding "their" puppet characters in 1986

Sarita and Maritza in their office at STAR

Once again Sarita and Maritza Segura wrote scripts—this time from offices at STAR. Maritza also developed the Teacher's Guide for the classic *Lugar Secreto* series.

Carlos and Amanda Luna moved from Colombia to the STAR studios, too, to puppeteer and to duplicate programs on DVDs. They both have incredible servant spirits and they willingly pitched in to help in any and every capacity.

Amanda, Carlos and Paulita

We began a new series for adolescents, *El Nuevo Lugar Secreto* (*The New Secret Place*), which Crysti (who returned as a missionary in her own right) produced, directed, and edited.

Sarita's scripts for the new series were poignant, insightful, and instructive, yet fascinating. They made us laugh and made us cry. We chose serious themes, suggested by Roberto Pérez, from 2 Timothy 3:1-5, and Sarita made the shows relevant to adolescents of this generation. The topics included *Unforgiveness, Self-Control, Gossip, AIDS, Disobedience, and Greed*.

The show on *Unforgiveness* featured a young teen who was embittered toward her father. She hated him so much that even when he was dying and sent her a letter begging for forgiveness, she would not go to visit him at the nursing home. Finally, she consented and approached the room where he lay dying. As she entered, he drew his last breath. She threw herself across his bed as she wept uncontrollably. Several weeks later, she visited his grave with a letter she had written to him, in which she asked for his forgiveness. By then, though, it was too late.

We finished shooting the death scene and broke for lunch. Everyone had tears in their eyes. After lunch, two interns from Colombia returned to the set to begin tearing down. When I walked in, the room was solemn. None of the usual banter and chatter. One of the interns slowly slid her arms under the father, lifted him gently, and reverently began to carry him out. He had just died. Never mind that he was a puppet.

***

Volunteers "bought" buildings in our newly constructed *Lugar Secreto* village. They built and decorated "their" restaurant, hotel, shoe shop, gazebo, general store, and kiosk.

RV-MAPS volunteers came to Durant to help for months on end. Wonderful people, including Cheryl and Bill Tomlinson, Myrt and Al Portinga, and Mary and Tom Bartolet. We were also blessed with MAPS appointees Mike and Judi Pinkerton, and Ed and Kim Baker. And, no doubt, things would have been in a mess without Edwina Hinson, our bookkeeper and office manager. Olan Hill conceptualized condensing *Secret Place* into packets of fifty-two programs, so that churches could use the shows for weekly ministry.

Judy and Steve Graner returned from Colombia for productions, along with William Bustos. John Taylor came from Honduras.

Nuevo Lugar Secreto set, built on 3-ft high platforms so that puppeteers can walk around in the entire village

Path where the puppeteers walk, plaza on right

Jamie Coad and William Bustos
resting for a moment beside the set

The Tampa Tribune Monday July 14, 1997

A Place for People, Puppets, and Cockroach Soup

Puppets at the restaurant (what the camera sees)

Restaurant set, actual (Joe is measuring with his arm
to check table height for a puppet)

For years I had wanted to produce a series on theology for adolescents because so many kids of that age "fall through the cracks" and are lost to firm Christian faith. Finally, I found the perfect book—*Meet God!* by John Higgins. Captivated by the concept and potential, I received permission to produce it on video. The task soon overwhelmed me, and I asked Crysti for help. The project developed a life of its own! She paired with Pastor Dan Betzer, and the world will never be the same! (Dan is our "old friend" and pastor of First Assembly of God, Ft. Myers, Florida.)

Dan is host and star of the show. He teaches from his "office set" to open and close the show. In-between—whew! you don't know what is coming next.

He plays eight different characters.

Dan, host-teacher, on the home-office set

He is **Dead-Eye Dan** with a black patch over one eye, the tough cowboy with a heart of gold.

Ed Baker running camera
John Taylor and Dead-Eye Dan

He is **Hermione Philpot,** the British Julia-Childs-wanna-be, who reigns with style and charm on her own cooking show.

Hermione on her kitchen set with Chris, make-up artist, and Greg, floor director

He is **The Maestro** music director in his canary yellow suit—flamboyant and flashy, directing crowds of people to sing better than they could ever have imagined.

El Maestro Dan

He is **Dan D. Deal,** selling you the worst used car for the best price you'll ever pay (his bad toupee is not included in the deal).

Dan D. Deal looking for a customer

He is **Miss Maude,** southern belle spinster librarian and fount of information, yet secret adventurer.

Miss Maude and Drew ride again

He is **Professor Dankenstein,** the brilliant scientist who resembles Albert Einstein, with thick glasses and a German accent.

Dr. Dankenstein

He is **Ben N. Shape** from a boxing career long ago and from a body far, far away.

Ben N. Shape working out with Trainer Brandon

Dozens of teens converged on the studio to participate in sketches. They became cast and crew and they scattered with our cameras to remote shoots.

Orientation before a shoot

William Bustos dubbing into Spanish
all the voices of Dan Betzer

We received criticism for being avant-garde on our approach to *Meet God!* (*Un Encuentro ¡con Dios!*). We were a little concerned—until we met Holly. Here is her story as told to us:

> When I was sixteen, my mom sent me from Ohio to live with my Aunt Lisa near Tampa. I was really messed up—I had been hanging around with the wrong crowd, which was sleeping around and experimenting with drugs and drinking.
>
> I hated everything. I hated my life. I decided to try, again, to kill myself. I curled up on the bed to figure out how to end my life.
>
> Aunt Lisa saw me and called her neighbor, a Christian. This woman came over, prayed with me, called a church counselor for an appointment for me, and left a video for me to watch.
>
> Later that evening, I started watching *Meet God!*. I could not believe it! That guy was so funny, and those teens were actually having fun. And I could tell they loved God a lot. This was the kind of kids I wanted to hang out with. I told Aunt Lisa, "I want to go to that church."
>
> The next evening the neighbor lady took me to her church (Assemblies of God on Turkey Creek Road in Plant City, Florida). It was Youth Night, and it was awesome. I asked Jesus into my life, and He radically changed me.
>
> Now I am baptized in water, and in the Holy Spirit, and I work with the youth group at "my" church. Thank you for literally saving my life.

A missionary emailed us from Athens, Greece. "We have a copy of your *Meet God!#1* … it has blessed us and the young people we work with in the International Church here in Athens … We are interested in ordering any new releases."

A Baptist youth pastor in Tampa told us, "Your host is very good. He really connects. His playing various roles helps the kids want to listen to the serious parts. The show is great. *Really* great."

Having fun on the set

Meet God! Secret Agents, of course
with Pastor Randy Helms

An angel pops In (with a microphone)

From France, "We watched the *Meet God!* at a meeting last Sunday night with the other missionaries, and everyone loved it! I found that watching our children captivated and interacting with the video was of special value to me. We have a group of seven MKs who were gathered to see it, from the ages of 5-11, and all the ages really responded well, including adults. All I can add is to tell you that we really need something like this to be translated into French and Arabic!!!!"

For both of our new series, *Nuevo Lugar Secreto* and *Meet God!* (*Un Encuentro ¡con Dios!*), we received emails and letters of "life change" from Guantanamo, Cuba; Venezuela; Ecuador; Mexico; Honduras; Costa Rica; Nicaragua; Paraguay; Chile; Colombia; South Africa; Fiji; Uganda; East Africa; U. S.; Philippines; India; France; Macedonia; Pakistan; Greece; Nigeria; Bolivia; and Spain. And also from Native Americans in Arizona and Alabama.

Sky Angel Satellite sent us an offering! "We wanted to bless you with a small gift of our appreciation for everything you do and for helping Sky Angel with our children's channel, KTV. You have been a real blessing and we appreciate it."

We were honored year after year by "The Communicator Awards" and the "Videography Award."

One of my favorite responses came from a student at Southwestern University, Waxahachie, Texas, after we had just participated in their Missions Week.

> My friends and I were talking about how awesome it is that you guys were on the cutting edge back in 1978 when you started STAR. To hear Dr. Guynes in chapel the other day—how he remembers being on the Foreign Missions Committee when they wondered what on earth to do with Brother Register and his dream of television production! And then to see the videos this week and to know you are still on the cutting edge, outside the box. That's what we want to be, outside the religious box, making the Gospel "connect" to a new generation. You guys at STAR are a real inspiration to us!

New productions flourished, but also, we needed to revitalize the old shows. That's when God sent Gene and Jeanne LaMay to STAR. They had been missionaries in Europe for twenty years. We teased them about being "Yankees" because they came from upstate New York. Now, Gene, a "computer tech," digitized new color into the original *Lugar Secreto* and *Secret Place* and also digitized the educational programs.

One of Gene's projects was to produce and direct a series of programs in Urdu. When Pastor Caleb and his friend Samuel arrived from the UK and began the pre-production with Gene, we learned that Urdu, similar to Hindi, is spoken in Pakistan and throughout the Middle East. Urdu Bibles are read from the back, Genesis is at the end of the book.

While Gene worked on pre-production, Jeanne designed and decorated the set. Then, as we would begin to shoot each 30-minute show, we would ask Caleb and Samuel if they needed anything before "rolling." "Yes," they inevitably answered, "Could we please have some more hot tea?" Jeanne ran back and forth between the kitchen and Studio B with the hot tea, honey, lemon, and cream.

> *Strange music filled the studio. The melody was haunting. The man's voice seemed a half-pitch off tone, following the melody line in Indian fashion. One dark-skinned man*

sat on the floor on a Persian rug; he beat rhythmically on two bongo-like drums, one large, and the other smaller. The second man stood beside a table, alternately pulling and pushing a wooden accordion-looking harmonium. He sang in Urdu. Both men swayed in time to the music, closing their eyes, looking heavenward, then looking into the video camera directly at the viewer, telling him about Jesus.

We marveled to think these programs would be broadcast by satellite into countries "closed" to the Gospel. And they would be duplicated hundreds of times onto DVDs. A viewer wrote to Pastor Caleb, "Jesus lives in your country. When you see him, will you tell him I want to meet him?"

Gene running camera on a remote shoot

Gene also ran camera hour after hour on remote shoots for the other productions.

Jeanne's skills are artistic, and so, besides running camera and decorating sets, she designed covers for the new DVDs. She learned to transfer the programs from the computer to the duplicating machine. Little did she realize that programs she duplicated would soon reach around the world on fourteen satellites.

In addition, Gene mentored college students who interned at STAR, teaching them computerized editing.

Gene, a master at Final Cut Pro

Seminar students from Latin America pose on the set

One of the interns to STAR that Gene mentored was Andrés Cuervo. Here is his story in his own words:

My dad, Carlos Cuervo, is a pastor in Colombia, South America. As a kid, I always "had" to go to church, and I really resented it. So, as an adolescent, I began to show my rebellion—I dressed all in black, with lots of chains hanging from my neck and waist. I was smart-mouthed and hung around with the wrong crowd.

When Dad announced special services for kids, I thought, "Oh, brother! Another booorrrring time of stupid stuff for little kids." Of course, I would attend the services. I had no choice. Dad made me go to church. The following Sunday, a man with reddish hair came as the evangelist. He said his name was Carlos Luna, and he was going to show us a video called *Lugar Secreto*. "Oh, man," I sighed, "Probably another hammy Christian video that will put me to sleep for sure."

The opening to the video was not too bad, and then an orangish-yellow, fuzzy puppet (of all things!) appeared. Bobo, they called him. He was so funny! I could not believe my eyes or ears! I was mesmerized! At the end of the video Bobo was sorry for all his mischievousness and repented by praying a simple prayer. Without thinking why not, without remembering all the reasons I hated church and religion, my heart prayed along with Bobo. My life was transformed from that moment.

Sobered, decent-acting now, I talked with Carlos at length. Turns out he was a character on the shows! He actually helped produce these videos! Right then, I determined that "when I grow up" I want to produce this type of quality Christian shows.

I followed my dream through high school, and then signed up for *YWAM* (Youth With a Mission) and was assigned to their video department in Puerto Rico. But, I kept *Lugar Secreto* in the back of my mind. Where is their studio located? What if I could visit there? And, possibly, even, be an intern there?

As soon as my visa allowed entrance to the United States, I contacted *STAR* and headed for the studio. Gene, a techi like me, took me under his wing. He showed me the *Final Cut Pro* editing program. He taught me one-on-one editing techniques.

Joe presenting internship certificate to Andrés

And so, on September 29, 2003, after completing my internship, this is what I wrote to the *STAR Media* Family:

It has been a privilege for me to serve by your side. The time with you has helped me know even better the heart of God and how He entrusts so much to those who serve Him. For years you have done what adults did not take seriously: reach the current generation "in their own language." You are bearing fruit and being multiplied through me into even more people. STAR is a ministry formed by people willing to take risks, adventuresome in heart, and ready to gain new territory for God, expending their lives to do so. This is so that the little children can come to Him without someone telling them, "Go away. He doesn't have time for you."

Thank you for giving me the opportunity to learn so much about the quality and excellence you put into each program. You give more than most people would think of giving even when they would consider it "the extra mile."

I think God is going to send more young people your way. They will be hungry to learn and eager to receive your guidance, and your passion for media and communications.

With much love,
Carlos Andrés Cuervo

South African seminar students
with missionary David Betzer and our STAR crew
(Gene holding the camera)

Joe, Maritza, Maggie, Sarita

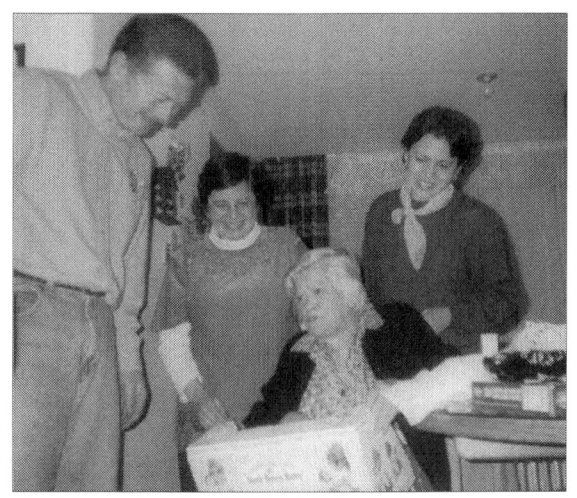

Doug (Crysti's husband) in Colombia with
Maritza, Sarita and their Mamá Cecilia

Jeanne, Amanda, Maggie, Paulita

A Place for People, Puppets, and Cockroach Soup

Brandon, Jennifer, Danielle, Kyndal
faithful cast and crew of *Meet God!*

Bobo relaxing at home, with his dog, Punkin,
newspaper, and coffee

Maggie and Fredda

William, the puppet Grandpa (driving the mower),
and Ed getting ready for an outside shoot

Marla is Bobo's right hand helper.

John Taylor, Tim, and Crysti
ready for a pre-production meeting

Carlos, John, Jero, William, and Amanda
on a *Nuevo Lugar Secreto* set

Students working on a script with Gloria Jackson

32

Bobby

A Half-Way House

"Hey, Bobby. How can I help you?" Joe asked from his desk. Bobby stood in the doorway, a confused look on his face. "Where are the stairs?" he inquired.

Joe got up, walked to the door, stepped out into the hallway, and pointed, "Down there, at the end of the hall. See? That's the door to the stairwell."

Bobby nodded, and ambled toward the door.

For the third time that morning, Bobby had asked and Joe had replied, as if it were the first time. Joe was incredibly patient and respectful with Bobby. We had known Bobby and Gloria Jackson since college days and actually had begun our missionary careers together in the summer of 1967.

Bobby and Gloria served as missionaries in Africa and Europe for 28 years. Then, in his late fifties, Bobby began to show behavioral symptoms that were cause for concern. He often became disoriented. He could no longer complete tasks that he had formerly carried out with ease. His visual perception appeared to be altered. Bobby's diagnosis was not good: early-onset Alzheimer's—devastating news to a couple whose appointment books were already filled for the next several months with ministry activities in Europe.

This tragedy intertwined with a severe crisis in the life of the couple's special-needs adult son, Brian—a crisis requiring their extended involvement in his care. Bob and Gloria (mostly Gloria) needed a new, stateside place of service in missions and STAR received them with open arms.

(Later, Gloria would write and *Life Publishers International* would publish—her book on suffering, *Through the Fire*: *Suffering as an Integral Component of Christian Life and Ministry*. This comprehensive biblical theology of suffering is accompanied by a study guide developed by Juanita Cunningham Blackburn, Gloria's longtime missionary colleague, who also served both in Africa and in Brussels. Both of these publications are available at the website *throughthefireministry.org*.)

Gloria and Bobby while at STAR

Although Bobby was already showing signs of impairment, he continued to travel to churches with Gloria on weekends doing deputational work. Even though he had just come to STAR, Bobby enjoyed helping to set up the display of products. And he was so pleased each week to bring back to STAR the money gained from the sale of the *Secret Place* programs!

Bobby was not given any direct responsibilities at STAR, but we gave him an office so that he would feel he was a vital part of the work. He had a desk and a sofa on which he could rest. Frequently, he would walk down the hallway, pop his head into the various offices, smile, and make simple remarks. Obviously, he wanted to be an "encourager" to each of us.

The summer after Bob and Gloria joined the STAR team, when the youth descended on the premises for the *Meet God!* and *Nuevo Lugar Secreto* "shoots," I was concerned about how everyone would treat Bobby. I need not have worried! For everyone treated him with respect and dignity, affectionately calling him "Uncle Bobby."

Uncle Bobby with his basket of snacks

"Uncle Bobby, I sure would like a snack," called a teen from under the puppet set. "Me, too, Uncle Bobby," yelled another kid from under the set in another part of the studio. Bobby grabbed his basket of goodies and shuffled to the set.

***

Not only did STAR enable youth to intern at the studio, STAR also became in a sense a "Half-way House." Bob and Gloria were not the first missionaries to find refuge, respect, and responsible ministry at STAR. Numerous times, missionaries were assigned to

STAR when they were in transition. Sandra Bass found a place of ministry between living in South America and becoming Women's Ministries District President in North Carolina and later in the South Texas District. Janie Boulware-Wead gained confidence and continued ministry between her time of service in Spain and her career in church planting and teaching. Gerald (Bobby's brother) and Gerri Jackson were invaluable, a tremendous blessing to STAR between their ministry in Europe and his becoming head of MAPS Construction in Springfield, helping to facilitate construction projects for national churches around the world. Eldon and Sue Brown developed the procedures manual and designed and decorated sets while they transitioned between Asia and Europe. Carlos Diaz, college student, blessed us with his engineering skills before he became a missionary in Europe.

The STAR staff welcomed each person and, hopefully, smoothed the transition to an even greater ministry.

One of the final tasks Bobby could do—even when his verbal skills were faltering—was to serve by picking up the trash, and he did that with great commitment. He held a big, black garbage bag and walked from office to office, offering the bag, nodding to everyone, wanting to "help." We would quickly try to find some trash to put in the bag, even if this was the second or third time that day that he had made the rounds.

As Bobby's condition continued to decline, he could not fully participate in the discussions at staff meeting. But one morning, when we had been discussing whether or not to act on some pressing problem, suddenly Bobby piped up, "Well, I always say, if you need to do something, *do* it!" We died laughing, and "did it"!

One of the most meaningful contributions that Bobby made to STAR was his prayers for God's direction and blessing. Despite his limited ability to express himself in normal conversation, he continued to pray very moving prayers in our staff meetings for the progress of the kingdom of God through STAR.

As Bobby's disease progressed, Gloria could no longer care for him at home. She found a nursing home between the studio and their home and stopped every evening to spend time with him. On Bobby's birthday, the entire STAR team descended on the nursing home with a big birthday cake and included everyone in the Alzheimer's unit in the celebration.

Sometimes when we visited Bobby, he would be preaching in French, or he would be praying loudly for a room full of residents. One day, during a lucid moment, Bob said to Gloria, "Honey, we've got to tell the whole world that we love Jesus!"

And those words quite succinctly describe the spirit of the entire succession of "transitioners" that made their way through STAR on their way to new ministries. They were all people facing challenges that could have stopped them in their missions journey. But they did not quit—they were all propelled by that same unquenchable drive to tell the whole world about the love of Jesus.

Bobby left a strong impact on us all, including the young people who worked with us in the production of the *Meet God!* series. My granddaughters, Jennifer and Kyndal, were adolescents while Bobby and Gloria served at STAR. As I was writing this book, Jennifer called me one day and said, "Do you have a chapter for Uncle Bobby in your STAR book? He needs to be featured."

Watching Bobby transition to heaven was not easy because he did not move on to another fulfilling ministry someplace else in the world. His weakened body was transitioning to its heavenly home. But, then, aren't we all in transition? Never certain of what tomorrow may bring?

"JESUS LOVES ME, THIS I KNOW..."
"CRISTO ME AMA, BIEN LO SE..."

33

Mario

Trust in the Lord ... lean not on your own understanding.
Proverbs 3:5

On a routine morning in 2003 Joe sat at his computer to open his email. There was a note from our boss which began:

> It is my duty to inform our colleagues at STAR that ... STAR will be discontinued in its present operations effective January 1, 2005 ... Of course a priority now will be to bring closure to any projects that are in development ... You are all aware, of course, of a different paradigm being created that will be based ... in the Ft. Lauderdale area ... I know that there are ministries at stake, that various ones could be disappointed or possible [sic] angry or hurt, or that supporting pastors and churches may be unhappy. That has all been taken into consideration ... I also realize that this action to discontinue is in contrast with my own earlier position that STAR would continue... I ask your collective forgiveness....

Shocked, in deep pain, we did not know what to do! Joe convened an emergency meeting of the staff and read the email to them. Everyone sat in stunned silence. Do we fight the edict? Roll over and play dead? The great question on everyone's mind was "Why?"

Our District Superintendent, Terry Raburn, tried to turn the tide ... to no avail. The Assistant Superintendent, Dan Betzer, emailed our headquarters and called and cajoled ... to no avail.

We never received an answer as to why. There was no moral failure. No misuse of funds. (On February 12, 2004, we calculated the cost per potential viewer at .0017 cents.) There was no impropriety of any kind. And the "different paradigm" referred to in the email from our boss never did develop.

We eventually learned that a national brother whom we had befriended and who had come to work with the crew at STAR told lies and half-truths to our superiors. This national brother so stirred up his friends back in his native country that they contacted our headquarters to tell how he was being mistreated, undervalued at STAR. In actuality, this brother at one point challenged Joe to leave and go raise funds while he ran *everything* at STAR. But, although he was capable in television production, his attitude was arrogant and overbearing. No one wanted to work "under" him. He especially despised Crysti. She knew how to edit on the new digital equipment, and he did not. Unfortunately, he did not want to learn how—he only wanted to supervise.

The stories of how this brother's attitude poisoned a missionary to join him in secret emails of betrayal are still, now, too painful for me to re-live.

***

Once again, *STAR Media Ministries* closed. In 2005 the facilities reverted to the local church, which uses them to this day.

Years later, we learned that a number of other older missionaries nearing retirement age, as we were, received similar notifications.

I know God is in control. I know He is sovereign. But his ways are certainly "past finding out," as the Bible says. I don't like to be pruned! I don't even like to *eat* prunes! But, deep inside, I know that God *causes good things* to result when we are forced to change, to give up our plans, to alter course.

***

An entrance to the STAR building

Once again, Paul Garber asked us to work with him—we had come full circle! Paul had gone to Europe as a missionary and had returned to work with Bob D'Andrea, founder of Channel 22 in Clearwater, Florida, where we had began our television ministry.

This time we moved to West Palm Beach, Florida, where Channel 22, now the *Christian Television Network (CTN)* with fourteen stations as well as channels on DirecTV and Dish Network, was beginning a satellite ministry called *Christian Television Network international (CTNi)*.

Joe, Peruvian brother, and Paul in Peru
making sure the satellite dish receives CTNi

Paul and Joe in Peru
being welcomed with music and dancing

Paul began airing *Lugar Secreto* as soon as the new satellite signal could be transmitted, and Bobo shot new short segments, *Pregúntale a Bobo*, talking to the kids. Paul asked me to tape a series of devotionals in Spanish for adults. Plus, Joe was invited to preach in a number of Latino churches.

We loved the international flavor of West Palm Beach, and the year we spent there was both healing and calming to our spirit. We lived in a typical West Palm neighborhood—a gated community comprised of a series of Mediterranean-style apartment buildings surrounded by towering palm trees, flowering hibiscus bushes, and rustling banana trees. Our apartment was on the third floor, and our only access was an open-air, broad staircase.

The ground floor apartment, adjacent to the stairs, was rented by a mean-looking Puerto Rican biker. Every afternoon when we came home from the TV station, we could hear the sound of a Harley revving even as we pulled into the apartments' parking lot. The biker wore baggy jeans, leather boots, a "wife-beater" undershirt, a wide leather bracelet, and had a brightly colored bandana on his head. His face reflected his rough life: flattened nose from having been broken, and a jagged scar that ran down his left cheek and continued under his scraggly beard. On his huge, muscular arms, tattoos glistened with the sweat of his exertion as he worked on the bike. He was so scary looking that I avoided eye contact. But not Joe.

Every afternoon, Joe would pause and greet the guy in Spanish. And, little by little, as the conversations lengthened, Joe learned that "Mario" had been in prison because he had killed a guy in a drunken fight. Self defense, Mario stated matter-of-factly. After several months of conversations, Joe invited Mario and his wife to go to the local Spanish church with us. And Mario accepted!

So, one Sunday morning, we waited for Mario to come out of his apartment. Startled, I could not stop myself from grinning at him—his boots were polished, his jeans were clean, and his aftershave (on his long beard) scented the courtyard. But best of all—his dress shirt: a black, see-through-net-with-sequins.

We got in the car and drove to the church, which was located in a shopping plaza. Mario said he had seen this place, but thought it was a doctor's office. I worried that people might look at us a little strangely ... but instead, they were wonderful. Everyone greeted Mario and his wife with courtesy, warmth, and respect. The pastor's sermon, about Lazarus "becoming alive after having been dead," was outstanding. And when the pastor extended an invitation to accept Christ as Savior, both Mario and his wife, with tears streaming down life-weary cheeks, went forward!

What a joy to see first-hand God's life-changing power! Once again, I was reminded that God's hand is at work in *all things*; for Mario's sake—if for nothing else—we had moved to West Palm.

And also, at the CTNi television studios, which we shared with Mike Gonzalez and the team at Channel 61, WFGC, we could see all of our former productions "continuing their life" on satellite after satellite, until they now have a potential Hispanic viewing audience of 7,000,000—reaching children and touching world-weary adults like Mario.

***

Of course, God knew that STAR would be closed; that's why He sent Gene and Jeanne LaMay from Europe to join the ministry at STAR. I marvel at the ministry they continue—distributing thousands of programs since STAR "closed"!

Tears fill my eyes as I listen to the new audio programs for children that Gene and Jeanne are now sponsoring. Dramas, written by our dear Sarita, that she and Maritza and Carlos and Amanda and William are recording digitally in their puppet voices in Colombia. Their children "do voices" now, too. The ministry goes on!

Every day missionaries of many denominations play DVDs in Spanish, English, Tamil, and Hindi to hundreds of expectant children whose eyes dance with eagerness to see Bobo and Judy and Cristina and Tomasito and Rosita … children who open their hearts to learn about God's love through Jesus. The ministry goes on!

Every day another generation sees Bobo from fourteen satellites, in 200 countries. The ministry goes on!

Wow—God certainly continues to have *A Place for People and Puppets* in bringing the Good News of Jesus, His Son, to the world.

Think of it! He continues to use the contributions of that "great company of volunteers"—including Pastor Waldron, Fredda, Eva, Paul, Juan, Bob, John, Sue, Cristina, David, Maritza, Sarita, Carl, Bruce, Roland, Evelyn, Hilda, Red, Tim, Toni, Dottie and Ken, Neil, Judy, Ana, Carol, Gene and Jeanne, and a host of others, some of whom have already left this world for heaven.

The ministry that God confirmed in the heart of Joe Register that evening when he stood on a balcony at twilight in Caracas, Venezuela and looked out at televisions being turned on in one of the city's poorest *barrios*—that ministry continues!

May God be praised! To God alone be the glory.

The coloring book in Spanish

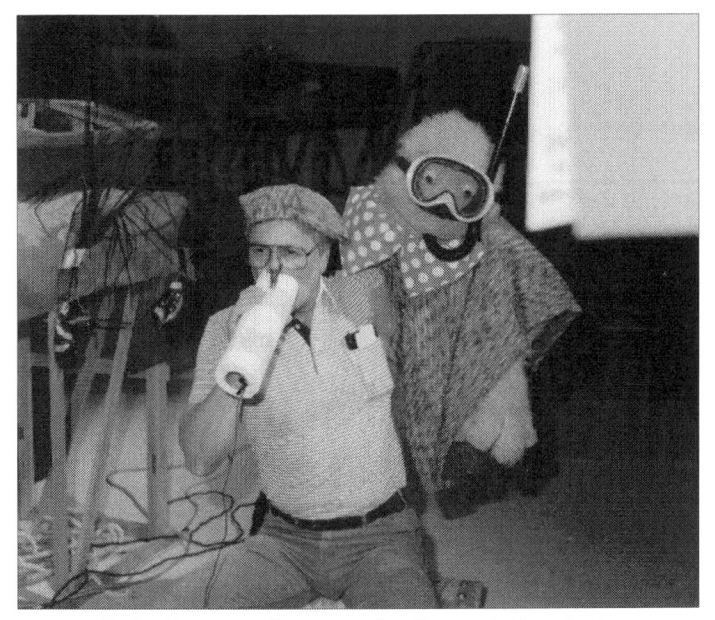

Bobo is preparing to swim through the shot.
Joe needs to get the sound of a snorkel just right.

Two guys resting after many hours of hard work

A Word from Joe

The Bible says in Hebrews 11:8 "By faith Abraham, when called ... obeyed and went even though he did not know where he was going." That is what I have endeavored to do, and I certainly did not know what I was getting into!

My God-given dream beginning back in 1977 was to produce videos, Spanish television for all of Latin America—something the Assemblies of God World Missions division had then never even considered.

My dream was "outside the box," "cutting edge." One of the men on the Missions Board told me later that they discussed how "crazy" my dream was.

It was a God-sized dream. I had to push, to persevere, even to get permission to "try" the dream.

When we produced our first series of *Lugar Secreto* (*Secret Place*) children's programs, Christian television in Spanish, for children, was unheard of. Impossible. Never been done before. Today those shows are literally around the world. Today they are reaching the third generation.

I am humbled to think that God chose me to develop such a far-reaching idea, that God took His plan and wrapped it in my dreams and hard work to reach countless children and adults around the world. I made many mistakes along the way, but mistakes don't scare God—He gave me mercy and grace and the resolve to keep going forward.

God will also give YOU a dream. A God-sized dream. Ask Him to put His dream in you. He will give you ideas that no one else has even thought of. Don't be discouraged by small-minded people. Persevere. Follow your God-given dream wherever it takes you—outside the box, in cutting edge evangelism—even though you don't know where you are going!

The back cover of the English *Secret Place* Coloring Book

Postlude

Retired now, with our great-grandchildren on our knees, Joe and I go on with ministry in English and in Spanish.

At the request of Pastor Scott Pfingston, we have helped to begin a Spanish church, *La Roca,* at Willow Oak Assembly of God in Mulberry, Florida. Jerónimo Pérez, Jr. and his wife, Angie, are our Spanish pastors. Jero and Angie lead and we help them as our health permits.

And we've helped to form a band of retired musicians to give concerts at luncheons and special events. Joe plays the saxophone and I play the keyboard. Bob Bushey, a retired teacher, plays the drums. Elmo Shareski from Manitoba, Canada, plays the bass guitar. And, sometimes, Ann Mabry plays the stand-up bass. Seniors love the old songs we play and sing, such as, "Just a Closer Walk with Thee" and "What a Friend We Have in Jesus."

Both Crysti and Tim continue to work in television production. Crysti teaches *Creative Communications to Children* and *TV Productions for Children* at Southeastern University (SEU), Lakeland, Florida. She has also taught the SEU video editing class on Final Cut Pro. Crysti and Doug's older daughter, Jennifer, and her husband, Wesley Morris, are ministers of music at Gulf Coast Church in Largo, Florida. Jen and Wes have two little, mischievous boys, Caden and Benson. Crysti's younger daughter, Kyndal, also married a Morris—Caleb—no relation to Wes. Kyndal and Caleb have a delightful daughter, Kaybree, and another little girl on the way.

Tim and his wife, Ashley, recently moved back to Florida from Washington, D.C., where he had served as Director of Multimedia for the non-profit educational entity, Association for Supervision and Curriculum Development (ASCD). Tim's skills on Final Cut Pro, and its forerunner "the Cube," brought us into the digital editing age. Tim has now joined the production company, *NFocus,* as a partner and is heading up the new Tampa office. (www.getnfocus.com) Tim's daughter, Tessa, an amateur photographer, is a senior at Lakeland High School and also a freshman in college.

I am very thankful to God for the wonderful friends who helped to make this book become a reality. The editing skills of Juanita Cunningham Blackburn make my stories say what I intended them to say and just didn't know quite how to phrase it. All errors are mine—I added them when Juanita wasn't watching. Every person who appears at length in this book replied to my emails and added details. Thank you.

I thank God for my husband, Joe, and all of my family who receive as a legacy all the joys and sorrows I have written about here. A special thank you to our daughter, Crysti Porter, who provided photos, remembered details, and added anecdotes. Tim Register, our son, creatively designed the cover for this book (as well as the cover for my first book *No Place for Plastic Saints: Earthquakes, Chicken Feet, and Candid Confessions of a Missionary Wife*). Thank you again, Tim.

What joy it will be to arrive in heaven and meet the people who laughed and then prayed with Bobo, Cristina, and Judy—people who accepted Jesus Christ as the only way to be saved from their sins.

And so, now, especially, I want my children and grandchildren and great-grandchildren to know that no man can thwart God's will for a person's life. Man can thwart what we *perceive* as God's will. But God's will for you, for me, is character growth, and no one can thwart that!

May you, Dear Reader, be blessed as you remember God's faithfulness to ordinary people whom He uses to accomplish His eternal purposes.